BASIC ILLUSTRATED

Bike Touring and Bikepacking

BASIC ILLUSTRATED

Bike Touring and Bikepacking

Justin Lichter and Justin Kline

FALCONGUIDES

GUILFORD, CONNECTICUT
HELENA, MONTANA

An imprint of Rowman & Littlefield
Falcon, FalconGuides, and Outfit Your Mind are registered trademarks of Rowman & Littlefield.

Distributed by NATIONAL BOOK NETWORK

British Library Cataloguing in Publication Information Available

Library of Congress Cataloging-in-Publication Data

Lichter, Justin.
 Basic illustrated bike touring and bikepacking / Justin Lichter and Justin Kline.
   pages cm
 Includes index.
 "Distributed by NATIONAL BOOK NETWORK"--T.p. verso.
 ISBN 978-1-4930-0968-8 (paperback : alk. paper) -- ISBN 978-1-4930-1923-6 (e-book) 1. Bicycle touring. I. Title.
 GV1044.L53 2015
 796.6'4--dc23
                              2015022342

♾™ The paper used in this publication meets the minimum requirements of American National Standard for Information Sciences—Permanence of Paper for Printed Library Materials, ANSI/NISO Z39.48-1992.

Contents

It is by riding a bicycle that you learn the contours of a country best, since you have to sweat up the hills and coast down them. Thus you remember them as they actually are, while in a motor car only a high hill impresses you, and you have no such accurate remembrance of country you have driven through as you gain by riding a bicycle.

—Ernest Hemingway

Introduction

The sensation of exploring and traveling by bike is like no other. Suddenly a daily ride can become an overnight adventure, a week-long vacation, a month-long escape, an open-ended expedition, and so much more. We have all experienced the excitement of travel—the unknown, new people, places, and experiences—but adding the element of a bicycle into the travel equation brings the experience, possibilities, and rewards to heightened levels.

Traveling by bike allows you to connect with your environment—feel the weather, experience the surroundings, deal with adversity, and bond with locals who would otherwise be strangers. While riding, you are naturally traveling at a speed that allows you to absorb your surroundings. Rather than just observing the environment, you experience its every element. You establish an instant connection with the road surface and gradient, natural elements of Mother Nature, scents of the surroundings, and local culture. In some cases these elements can provide some of the most euphoric experiences, and in other cases they may provide the greatest level of adversity you'd care to experience. Regardless of which, you'll feel more alive, and we can guarantee the result will be a vivid memory that your mind and body can recall from multiple senses.

We have been fortunate to travel tens of thousands of miles under our own power, predominantly by bike and foot, to some of the most amazing destinations around the world. This book provides a culmination of our experience on the bike and in the backcountry, and is designed to provide you with the foundation and inspiration to set out on an overnight journey by bike.

In the pages that follow, we'll review basic cycling and camping gear, packing and traveling techniques, backcountry skills, and tips from the road that will save you time, money, and energy before heading out on your first, or next, bike tour. You'll find this Basic Illustrated Guide not only provides a foundation for bike touring and bikepacking skills, but also serves as a reference tool for seasoned cyclists.

Now let's talk more about the road ahead and get one step closer to turning the pedals.

—Justin Lichter aka Trauma and Justin Kline

Remember to pack it in, pack it out, tread lightly, take only pictures, and leave nothing more than faint tire tracks by practicing Leave No Trace outdoor ethics. Visit LNT.org.

CHAPTER ONE

Types of Touring

Road Touring

Road touring can be a great introduction to bicycle travel since you can have access to many of the comforts of home and often remain within cell phone service in case you have a repair or other issue you can't deal with. A tour or bikepacking trip on the road is easily accessible out your front door and can be an opportunity to travel to places that would have otherwise been done by car. Even when touring routes you have previously driven, you'll find the experience by bike to be far different and provide new perspectives to even a familiar landscape.

There is no denying the excitement of exploring the open road by bicycle. BETH PULITI

If camping is not for you, then "credit card touring" can be an ideal option. This involves carrying minimal gear and food, utilizing towns throughout the day to stop for meals, and ending the day at full-service accommodations. This shaves weight and items from your kit since you can do without a sleeping system, shelter, or having to carry much food. Even in remote areas of the United States, it is hard to go over 150 road miles without coming across a town or convenience store.

Bike Selection

The great thing about bike touring is that it can be easy to enjoy with equipment you likely already own, especially when touring on pavement. Bike options are plentiful, so developing a better idea of your budget, planned routes, and desired style of touring will help narrow the focus. Typically the best starting point for selecting a bicycle for road bike touring is taking an honest assessment of how much weight you plan to carry on your journeys. If you are a lightweight traveler carrying only the necessities, then a traditional road bike is a solid choice to keep consistent with your ultralight mantra. If you consider yourself someone who packs for the occasion, enjoys a few of the comforts of home, and brings along those just-in-case items, then a dedicated touring bike will be best suited to handle the weight of your cargo.

Road Bikes

Touring on a traditional road bike enables you to travel quickly and easily, assuming you are carrying minimal gear and traveling a nicely paved route. Skinny tires ensure minimal rolling resistance, and drop-style handlebars offer several hand positions and an overall aerodynamic position while on the bike. Road bikes, especially those designed for racing, are crafted from the lightest weight materials available and are often equipped with ultralight wheels, making the pedaling as effortless as possible. For competitive endeavors these attributes are ideal, but the weight savings on the bike sacrifices features and durability that you may require for longer touring pursuits.

For ultralight paved tours and short overnight journeys, a road bike is a worthwhile consideration, especially if this is already what you own and you are looking to expand your rides beyond a single day. Just be conscious of the amount of weight you plan to carry and the limitations of your road bike.

Pros:
Lightweight
Commonly available at bike shops
Fastest type of bike for smooth surface riding

Road bikes are lightweight and fast on the road, but may lack comfort and carrying ability for longer tours. JUSTIN KLINE

Cons:
Geometry is not as comfortable as a touring bike
Wheels are not built to carry extra weight
Most road bikes lack fender and rack mounts

Tip: If shopping for a road bike, look for a model that does more than just road racing. Small details like extra water bottle bosses and fender mounts will go a long way as your rides start taking you overnight and farther from home.

Touring Bikes

Bikes designed specifically for touring offer an abundance of useful features for traveling for an extended period of time. Touring bikes are designed to carry heavy loads while remaining stiff and durable, and have geometry that promotes all-day comfort. Think of a touring bike as the Cadillac of bicycle options—build for comfort and loaded with features. Racks, fenders, additional mounting options, and even replacement spokes are some of the bells and whistles that can be found on stock touring bikes. Frame materials are chosen for durability over weight, so steel is a common building block. Able

A touring bike, such as the Raleigh Sojourn, is equipped to hit the road right out of the box. Here, a front rack was added for extra carrying capacity and versatility. Justin Kline

to withstand impact and be easily re-welded if cracked, steel is a hard material to beat for affordable, long-term touring durability. Just keep in mind that features and durability all add up on the scale. Be aware, especially when shopping price point touring bikes, that their combination of intended durability and entry-level components can make for some of the heaviest offerings on the market.

Pros:
Typically fully equipped right out of the box (some even come with
    replacement spokes)
Comfortable geometry
Long-haul durability

Cons:
Availability and size options may be limited
Often heavier than road or cyclocross options
Can be less than ideal for other types of cycling

Tip: Be aware of the numerous shifting styles on touring bikes. They can range from STI (integrated shifter and brake levers), to bar-end, to downtube. While STI is preferred in the road racing world, the durability and ease of maintenance of bar-end shifters is a reliable choice for long-distance touring cyclists.

Tip: Don't be afraid to look beyond the major brands. Companies like Trek, Specialized, and Giant dominate most of what you will see when walking into a bike shop, but little of their attention is devoted to touring models. There are many smaller brands and custom frame builders that focus their designs and innovations around touring and exploration by bike.

Additional Bike Options

Cyclocross Bikes

A cyclocross bike is aesthetically similar to a road bike, and shares the common attribute of drop-style handlebars, but with slightly different geometry. Originally designed for cyclocross racing, "cross" bikes can make for an excellent touring rig since they are lightweight, accommodate larger tires than road bikes, and often accept a variety of gear-carrying options.

Pros:
Good balance of lightweight and versatility
Larger tire clearance
More available models with disc brakes

Cons:
Slower than a road bike on pure pavement routes
Racing-inspired geometry is less comfortable on long trips compared to a
        touring bike
Racing models have limited or nonexistent water bottle mounts

A cyclocross bike can prove to be a versatile bikepacking rig. Justin Kline

Adventure Bikes

An emerging category within the world of bikes these days is adventure bikes. The premise is a bicycle that is designed to do just that, take you on an adventure that could be an all-day ride or travel lasting an extended period of time. Adventure bikes are not only being developed to cover a variety of terrain, but also focus on weight savings and ride quality, and therefore are becoming an evolving category outside of the rigid classifications of road, touring, cross, and mountain bikes. In addition to versatility and touring-specific features, geometry is what notably sets these bikes apart from typical road and cross bikes. With an emphasis on all-day riding comfort and capability to handle varied terrain, adventure bikes have a more stretched-out wheelbase, lower bottom bracket height, and a more relaxed head tube angle.

Pros:

Good option for a single do-it-all bike
Features and geometry designed specifically for touring and bikepacking
Most options for water bottle mounts

Cons:

Likely overbuilt if you are a lightweight traveler sticking to pavement
Category is still in its infancy, so options are limited and still evolving
Geometry can be limiting when riding primarily off-road

Adventure bikes like this Salsa Fargo come equipped with an abundance of tour-worthy features, such as a suspension seatpost, downtube water bottle mounts, and fork mounts for water bottles or oversized carrying cages. You'll also be able to find stock frame bags that provide a perfect fit within the main triangle as shown here. SALSA CYCLES

Recumbent Bikes

Another bike option, noted for its comfort characteristics and sometimes preferred in the brevet community, is the recumbent. A brevet is a long-distance cycling event, sometimes called randonneuring. Upon first glance a recumbent is notably different than traditional bike offerings. The idea is that a recumbent allows you to have a lower center of gravity and a more reclined

I had the chance to attempt riding a touring recumbent in Croatia. BETH PULITI

position while riding. The laid-back seating position creates less fatigue on body parts that typically experience stress while riding.

Pros:

Eliminates pressure points and strain on the groin area typically associated
    with long-distance cycling

Ergonomic design is more accommodating on your back, neck, and wrists

Can be faster than traditional bikes on flat ground and nontechnical descents

Cons:

Can be difficult to balance and unstable at slow speeds

Limited gear-carrying options compared to traditional bikes

Recumbents, along with proprietary parts, can be difficult to source and have
    limited availability, particularly while on-the-road touring.

Folding Bikes

A folding bike can be a great option for traveling shorter distances, particularly in urban areas. The compact design and small footprint open up new opportunities for traveling, particularly in congested areas or when utilizing multiple modes of transportation. Folding methods vary widely depending upon the manufacturer, so be sure to identify which model best accommodates your budget, weight, and size requirements.

Pros:

Will usually be considered checked luggage when flying without paying an
    additional handling fee

Ideal for traveling using varied methods of transportation (riding, bus, train, etc.)

Easy to store and keep safe in hotel rooms or even your tent

A folding bike can be a viable option for touring short distances and in urban areas. We met this cyclist (second from left) touring on his folding bike outside of Kuala Lumpur in Malaysia. BETH PULITI

Cons:

Small wheel size makes for slower going, particularly over a long distance

Less stable on high-speed descents

Folding bikes can also be difficult to source and have limited availability for replacement parts while traveling

Tandem Bikes

If your bike travels will be with a significant other, friend, or other companion, then a tandem is a worthwhile option to consider as well. When riding a tandem together, the otherwise solitary act of cycling can become a more social experience. The nature of a tandem also helps level the playing field between two cyclists of varying fitness levels, allowing the more skilled cyclist to do more work and captain the tandem, while the other cyclist can assume the role of the stoker.

Pros:

Fewer components and spare parts to worry about while traveling (compared to two bikes)

Faster on flat terrain and descending compared to traditional single bikes

Keeps you and your traveling partner in close proximity for easy communication

Cons:

Learning curve to starting, balancing, and maneuvering

Typically expensive and less common

Carrying capacity is less than traveling on two individual bikes, if relying on traditional panniers only

Carrying Methods for Road Touring

One of the beauties of road touring is that it provides the most carrying options over any other type of riding—from credit card touring with just a small handlebar bag to carrying an expedition-worthy amount of gear on the bike with a trailer in tow, and everything in between. All are viable options when you are on the road pedaling a suitable bicycle, so nailing down the option that is right for you will largely depend on your riding style and amount of gear you will be hauling.

Most road touring cyclists carry their load via panniers or trailer, which are both great options for bringing along a comfortable amount of gear. Either option will provide sufficient space without overloading, but deciding between the two is a matter of personal preference. For many, carrying gear on the bike with panniers is preferred, as it can provide a well-balanced load with predictable handling, but if keeping weight off the bike is your preference, then a trailer is a viable option. A trailer keeps all your gear in one place and allows you to easily detach your touring load and travel freely on side trips.

A touring handlebar bag like this one from Ortlieb provides convenient access to gear while touring on the road. BETH PULITI

Looking to go lighter? If covering more ground and turning the pedals over more easily are appealing to you, then trimming down your kit and carrying everything with frame bags is your best option. Without the additional weight and bulk of racks and panniers, your setup will be far lighter and even more aerodynamic, ultimately allowing you to use a lighter bike and wheels.

Additional Considerations for Road Touring

Wheel Size

Although less so these days, wheel size has been a debatable matter for bicycle touring setups. Typical road bikes utilize 700c (29-inch) diameter rims, while some touring-specific bikes are offered in either 26-inch or 700c wheels. The larger 700c road-based wheels are preferred for their increased rolling performance, but 26-inch wheels are sometimes still used by shorter riders or those traveling to remote regions abroad where the 26-inch platform is more common and thus easier to source replacement parts.

Bike Handling and Balance

Before you set out on your first overnight adventure, be sure to test the handling characteristics of your newly loaded bicycle. Disproportional weight distribution or poorly secured items can lead to sacrificed handling characteristics or a dangerous shimmy on climbs and especially descents.

While touring through central Italy, Mike demonstrates that even when carrying an abundance of gear, a bike can handle well if the weight is distributed evenly. BETH PULITI

Comfort

Overnight trips by bike mean longer days in the saddle and increased stress on pressure points. The saddle and related contact points are an obvious area to focus on, but do not overlook the cockpit of the bike. The majority of road touring setups rely on drop-style handlebars, which provide numerous hand positions on the drops, hoods, and flat portion of the bars. Alternating your hand positions throughout the day is more important when touring to avoid numbness and other fatigue issues with your hands, wrists, and neck.

Brakes

Be sure to evaluate the stopping performance of your loaded bike before hitting the road. The stock road or cantilever brakes may not be ideally suited for your bike once additional touring weight is added. Whenever possible we prefer to use disc brakes on all bikes. Disc brakes provide increased braking performance in all conditions and are unmatched in inclement conditions, such as rain and mud.

Gravel Road Touring

As road cyclists look for new challenges and adventurers look for more remote route options, cycling and touring on gravel roads, dirt roads, and other nonpaved roads ("gravel grinding") has become a growing segment in the world of cycling and bike touring. In fact, there are now a number of popular gravel road races throughout the country. Travel on these low-traffic roads is

The allure of gravel—challenging, traffic-free scenery and adventure. BETH PULITI

a rewarding experience providing new challenges, views of rural scenery, and often more abundant camping options at the end of a long day.

Expanding your touring horizons to include gravel roads is an easy transition, as the barrier to entry is relatively low. Often a dirt road tour can be completed on a bike you already own with a similar carrying method as used on the road. As mentioned previously in the Road Touring section, there's also a new category of adventure bikes designed specifically for mixed terrain riding that would be ideal for such conditions. Let's review bike options and some of the key points to consider when choosing a bike for gravel road touring.

Road Bikes

A road bike can be an okay option for gravel road touring provided the roads are well maintained, but road bikes typically lack sufficient tire clearance for a larger-width tire, so their performance is limited. The lightweight platform is a speedy option on well-maintained dirt and gravel roads, but when the road is pothole-ridden and plagued with the usual washboard sections, you are in for a harsh ride. Many road bikes often lack fender-mounting capabilities that could also leave you covered in unwanted grime at the end of the day.

Touring Bikes

Most touring bikes are well suited for both road and light gravel/dirt touring from the start. They accept larger tires than a road bike to provide additional comfort, and are also capable of accepting full fender coverage to keep you clean from the varied terrain. Touring bikes often provide easier gearing as well, which is appreciated for steep, loose, and more rugged terrain. With this typically comes a heavier overall weight, but a solid bike on unforgiving terrain is hard to beat.

Cyclocross Bikes

A cyclocross bike is an excellent choice for gravel road touring and exploration. Many cross bikes are exceptionally light and still provide clearance for wider and more aggressive tire treads. Cyclocross bikes are right at home on gravel, dirt, and other mixed terrain.

Adventure Bikes

Exploring and touring unpaved roads are what these bikes are designed for; they're well equipped for handling varied terrain with geometry that provides daylong comfort. Some of the options within this segment are being marketed for specific applications, but don't be afraid to explore options that provide a good fit for you, even if you aren't lining up for the next Great Divide Race.

Unpaved terrain requires larger-volume tires to keep the wheels rolling comfortably, or you'll likely find yourself jostled and constantly out of the saddle attempting to avoid discomfort. BETH PULITI

Aero bars, even on a mountain bike, can offer advantages when touring on gravel or dirt, such as easy map management, simple frame bag mounting underneath, and additional hand positions for comfort. JUSTIN KLINE

Mountain Bikes

A mountain bike is also a reasonable option for gravel/dirt touring, especially if you are doing so in more remote areas where roads are less maintained and potentially more rugged. In general a mountain bike can be slightly more sluggish on well-kept gravel paths, but the added comfort will be appreciated if the going gets rough. Mountain bikes are also made to handle rugged terrain, so maintenance is less of an issue over the long haul.

An ultralight bikepacking setup for an overnight gravel adventure. BETH PULITI

Carrying Methods for Gravel Touring

Just as with standard road touring, gravel road touring can be done with a wide variety of carrying methods, from rack and panniers or a trailer to bikepacking-style frame bags. Which one is best largely depends on the gravel/dirt conditions of your route and the amount of gear you are carting along. The biggest variable to consider, however, is the added fatigue on your setup from the unpaved surfaces. On rough roads rack bolts can vibrate loose (or even shear off), pannier mounts can break, and trailers provide an

Trouble in Turkey

When the road turns to dirt, as it often does in many alluring destinations, the level of fatigue on your bike and gear is elevated particularly on rigid mounting points. Recently a portion of my travels took me through Turkey, where the most interesting route seemed to be on remote gravel roads through small villages. Eventually the constant vibrations, combined with the weight of my load, were enough to snap my rear rack bolt in two. I was able to make it through the next two days with the help of a hose clamp, parachute cord, and several zip ties, but it was a reminder of the advantages of a rackless setup when traveling on rough roads. —Justin Kline

additional potential failure point, as well as a third wheel that can be punctured. For these reasons, and whenever traveling with minimal gear on gravel tours, frame bags are a great option to consider.

With a bikepacking-style frame bag setup, your kit is more agile and moves more freely with the bike in contrast to the rigid contact points of panniers and trailers. This ultimately allows you to travel more comfortably and quicker since you have less worry about gear and parts vibrating loose over extended gravel tours.

Additional Gravel Touring Considerations

Dust, Dirt, and Mud

The element of unpaved travel comes with a number of additional factors to consider before heading out on the bike. In dry conditions dust and dirt can be a notable variable, so it is helpful to have eyewear with lenses suitable for variable lighting to keep your eyes dust free. Dry dust and dirt can also quickly accumulate in your drivetrain, so be sure to keep your chain clean and be prepared with a chain lube for the appropriate (wet or dry) conditions.

While dust and dirt can be a nuisance, weather, particularly rain, can quickly change the dynamic of a tour on unpaved surfaces. Gravel washes away; water pools, making the depth of potholes indiscernible; and dirt quickly turns to mud that sticks to your tires or in some cases can stop you in your tracks.

A full-coverage fender will not only keep you dry in the rain, but it will also keep the dirt and dust off you and your gear. BETH PULITI

Ideally on a gravel/dirt road tour, your setup will have:

- Sufficiently wide tires—a minimum width of 28mm—are recommended to provide some float and comfort on gravel and rough dirt roads. For carrying a heavier load, consider a tire in the 32mm to 50mm range. More volume means more float over the rough stuff.
- Additional clearance between the tire and frame to prevent buildup of mud
- Front and rear fenders to keep dust, dirt, and mud off you and your kit

Flat Tires

Unlike smooth paved roads, dirt and gravel often present opportunities for flat tires around every bend. If you plan on embarking on a multiday gravel route, be sure to check the durability of your tires (road racing slicks are less than ideal) and come prepared with more patches and tubes than you might otherwise need on a typical road ride.

Bike Handling

With loose surfaces come additional bike handling challenges. Before undertaking an extended gravel/dirt tour, be sure you are accustomed to the handling characteristics of your bike on these unpredictable surfaces, particularly if you are on a road bike. For these same reasons it is important to ensure your gear is well-balanced and as stable as possible to avoid washing out on potentially loose surfaces.

Stock Up

Most unpaved roads are the way they are because they are lightly traveled, and the added expense of paving them is not justifiable by the local municipality. This presents great opportunities for mostly car-free riding, but it also means you are less likely to encounter services along the way. For multiday gravel/dirt tours be sure to stock up on needed supplies, such as food and water, and have a good idea of when you might have the opportunity to replenish.

Handlebar Bags

Touring-style handlebar bags are a convenient storage compartment for cameras, food, and other items used regularly throughout the day, but on rough gravel roads the contents can be taken on a ride resembling the spin cycle of a washing machine. Some models come with removable dividers, which unfortunately seldom stay in place when riding unpaved terrain. If your

While civilization may be less frequent on dirt and gravel tours, the buildings you do come across offer more character and sometimes provide public shelter, such as this cabin in New Hampshire. BETH PULITI

When touring unpaved surfaces with a rigid-mount handlebar bag, the contents will be jostled about. Be sure to secure precious cargo like digital cameras and fresh fruit harvests. JUSTIN KLINE

route entails large portions of gravel, be sure to pack handlebar bag contents tightly, and include additional soft items to take up any otherwise unfilled space.

Off-Road Touring

Singletrack and off-road touring is the ultimate backcountry escape. Traveling with just what you need, nothing less and seldom more, is a rewarding and invigorating experience. Off-road touring and bikepacking typically mean tackling technical terrain and more remote locations. Flowing singletrack, mountain vistas, and remote campsites are just some of the rewards you can encounter when departing on off-road overnight adventures.

Bike Selection

For off-road touring, bike selection can be largely dependent upon your route. Luckily you have no shortage of options these days, as almost any quality bike with sufficient tire width can take you on an overnight off-road adventure. A cyclocross bike, hardtail mountain bike, full-suspension mountain bike, or even a fat bike are all great options for an off-road tour.

A cross bike is an ideal choice for an off-road tour that is primarily double-track, fire service roads, logging roads, snowmobile trails (summer), or a trip that involves connecting sections of trail with road riding in between.

Tip: Look for a cyclocross bike equipped with disc brakes. The small additional investment will be well worth it when you hit the road or trail. Disc brakes offer superior stopping power, especially when carrying gear and in wet or muddy conditions.

Mountain bike choices are seemingly endless these days. In addition to choosing between a hardtail or full-suspension mountain bike, there are now several wheel sizes to choose from, which could be the subject matter of its own book. Major bike manufacturers are currently offering mountain bikes with 26-inch, 27.5-inch, or 29-inch wheels, with some companies choosing to focus exclusively on a specific wheel size or two. The basic theory behind the variation in wheel size offerings is that smaller wheels (26-inch) handle better, larger wheels (29-inch) roll faster and over obstacles easier, and the latest in-between wheel size (27.5-inch) is supposed to provide a solid balance between the two. Don't let the wheel size debate overwhelm you, though. Your best bet is to test-ride one or two for comparison, but the bottom line is that any wheel size is capable of getting you out on an overnight trip and putting a big smile on your face.

Choosing between a hardtail and a full-suspension mountain bike is an important decision and should be largely based on your riding style and the locations you plan to frequent on the bike. A hardtail provides the ultimate in efficiency and will typically be less expensive and lighter weight, depending upon the frame material. If you like to climb, ride less-technical terrain, prefer simplicity, or are looking to save weight, a hardtail could be your preferred steed. For those who live for the descent, prefer technical terrain, and are looking for a plush ride, then full suspension is highly recommended. Today's well-equipped full-suspension mountain bikes are incredibly efficient, fully adjustable, and capable of being fully locked out so you can really fine-tune the bike to your ride. Just remember, most of us are not lucky enough to be off-road touring on a daily basis, so be sure to choose a configuration that is going to suit your unloaded singletrack shredding needs, as well as when it comes time to strap the sleeping bag on and head into the wilderness for an overnight adventure. A dedicated mountain bike is the ideal choice for bikepacking on singletrack and rugged backcountry paths like the Great Divide mountain bike route and the Colorado Trail.

Tip: If you can only have one bike in your quiver, a larger-diameter wheel (27.5- or 29-inch) hardtail mountain bike is an excellent choice. The larger wheels will roll better on both dirt and paved surfaces, and a fork equipped with a lockout and lack of rear suspension ensure an efficient ride no matter what the terrain.

Fat bikes—the newest breed of mountain bikes—were originally designed for snow, sand, mud, and other extreme conditions. The aesthetics and sheer fun factor are expanding the segment, and fat bikes are becoming more commonplace for a variety of riding. As an emerging segment, fat bikes are opening up new possibilities of wilderness exploration by bike. They enable you to run incredibly low psi (pounds per square inch), allowing you more float over rugged, soft, and wet terrain. The penalty for this is increased rolling weight from oversized wheels and tires. In some cases a fat bike tire can weigh as much as the frame itself, so it is important to consider your intended use and options before committing to a fat bike. A fat bike is an ideal setup for winter bikepacking, coastline exploration, and overnight adventures

While fat bikes are not ideal on the road, they can be worth their added weight on mixed terrain routes. Shortly after this photo was taken, the pavement ended and the adventure began. Beth Puliti

Fat bikes are right at home in winter conditions and when the terrain promises to be rugged. BETH PULITI

through primitive, muddy, or soft terrain where the extra float of an oversized tire is required.

Tip: A second set of wheels can make a fat bike extremely versatile for year-round enjoyment. Eighty to 100mm rims are ideal for spreading your weight out during winter snow conditions, while a 29-plus wheelset can allow you to significantly cut down on rolling weight for three-season riding.

Carrying Methods for Off-Road Touring

Off-road touring is about enjoying the wilderness on your bike and getting the same trail riding experience that you would while riding unloaded. The best way to truly accomplish this is by minimizing your kit and carrying your gear in a traditional bikepacking fashion using frame bags. This type of setup keeps the weight of your gear balanced and allows you to remain nimble while navigating technical and twisty singletrack. You will appreciate the reduced weight while climbing and feel a noticeable performance difference on the trail, allowing your bike to retain its normal handling characteristics.

If you are truly unable to narrow your gear down enough to be carried in frame bags, then racks and panniers are another viable option for off-road touring. This will, of course, provide the added space you might need, but the sacrifice is additional weight, a wider load, and potentially compromised bike handling.

A trailer is another possibility for off-road touring if you are hauling gear for your family or a group on wider paths, but it is otherwise not an ideal off-road transport option, especially on singletrack. Maneuvering a trailer load can be difficult or almost impossible on tight, twisty singletrack.

This is an ideal setup for multiday bikepacking on singletrack or exploring other types of off-road routes. JUSTIN KLINE

Additional Off-Road Considerations

Suspension

While full suspension can be a luxury on technical trails, it does have its drawbacks when it comes to touring off-road. An air rear shock means pressure needs to be checked and air may need to be added on longer outings, thus requiring a shock pump. Rear suspension also becomes an additional potential failure point when touring off-road. A blown rear shock could be a trip ender if you are not prepared with a way to affix the bike with the suspension in the fully sprung position. And, if you are looking for the lightest option when it comes to bikes, a hardtail is typically the lightest choice.

Tubeless Tires

A flat tire can be the demise of an afternoon ride on the local trail, but that is not an option when it comes to touring off-road, especially in remote regions. To minimize punctures and pinch flats, running a tubeless tire setup can be a preferable off-road setup. The premise of a tubeless setup is to reduce the opportunity for flat tires by eliminating the tube. Without a tube inside the tire, pinch flats from trail obstructions are not possible and punctures from sharp objects are minimized thanks to a sealant designed to instantly fill any holes that might develop in the tire itself.

Here is a reasonably lightweight setup used for mixed terrain touring for several weeks in southeast Alaska. Fortunately the potential reliability issue of the rear suspension was not an issue. JUSTIN KLINE

If the advantages of tubeless sound ideal for your next cycling excursion, there are a few things you'll need to know to make the switch.

Wheels can be set up tubeless relatively easily by ensuring you have both a UST tubeless-ready wheel and tire. The compatibility of both ensures the most reliable seal and minimizes the chance of residual air leaking over time.

Alternatively, many standard wheels and tires can be converted to tubeless using a conversion kit of rim strips, tubeless sealant, and replacement valve stems. For details on the conversion process, visit notubes.com/detailed_kit_instruction.aspx.

Disc Brakes

Hydraulic disc brakes are often preferred on the trail riding scene, particularly for freeride and downhill pursuits, but when it comes to reliability and serviceability in the backcountry, mechanical disc brakes are the option of choice. No spare fluid, bleed kit, or proprietary components are required for mechanical disc brakes. An extra set of pads and brake cable will cover most of the needs for trailside servicing.

Cockpit Comfort

Touring/bikepacking in the backcountry often means increased vibration from rugged trails and increased fatigue on the body. Stock handlebars on mountain bikes are typically equipped with flat or riser-style handlebars, which are ideally suited for navigating singletrack on an unloaded bike, but consider altering the stock setup to deal with the additional strain from increased hours in the saddle and weight on the bike. Here are some options to minimize hand fatigue:

- Add bar ends to provide an additional hand position
- Wrap and tape additional padding over stock grips to provide more cushion
- Replace stock bars and/or grips with alternative styles designed to offer numerous hand positions and versatile mounting options for gear

Minimizing Weight

When your journey heads off the pavement, the weight of your load becomes even more important. Rough terrain, drastic changes in elevation, and narrow trails are commonly part of the off-road touring experience. With a lightweight and compact setup, you'll be better able to negotiate obstacles and fully enjoy the singletrack riding experience.

All loads are not created equally. Less gear weight can lead to a better riding experience when venturing into the wilderness. BETH PULITI

You never know what you might come across when exploring remote and seldom-traveled wilderness paths. BETH PULITI

Limited Restocking Options

Compared to other types of touring, bikepacking and touring on singletrack and long-distance off-road routes typically provide the least amount of resupply options. This means that within your carrying options you'll need to leave ample space for food and water. The good news is that on a bike you are able to cover far more ground than if you were hiking the same trail. For example, on a route like the Great Divide, which has limited services in some sections, you might be able to pedal 100-plus miles a day, allowing you to reach multiple towns during the course of the day. No matter what the route, though, know your options and how much food and water you will need to carry.

CHAPTER TWO

Carrying Methods for Bike Touring

The premise behind bike touring is simple: Gather what you need, attach it to your bike, and off you go. There is no better way to start than with the bike and gear you already own, and you'd be surprised how far you can get with what you already have access to.

There are a number of options when it comes to carrying your overnight gear on the bike, so evaluating these options will ensure you have the ideal setup for your journey, whether it is a sub-24-hour overnight jaunt or an around-the-world adventure. Touring setups have traditionally relied on carrying gear with a rack and panniers, a trailer, a backpack, or even combining a variety of these carrying techniques for increased capacity. Each carrying method has its place depending on the trip, and there are distinct advantages and disadvantages for each, so let's run through some carrying options in more detail.

Racks and Panniers

Racks and panniers are the most commonly used system for carrying gear on a bike. For overnight cycling trips this system provides a relatively simple carrying method that can accommodate a variety of gear configurations and load sizes. Racks and panniers are readily available through local bike shops and allow an abundance of gear to be transported while maintaining a balanced load when packed properly. Even without proper panniers, cyclists can simply strap bags or dry sacks to the top of racks and be on their way.

Pros: With front and rear racks and panniers, it is relatively easy to distribute weight evenly. This setup offers a large carrying capacity without being excessively bulky. Panniers can be easily removed and carried with you while

Racks and panniers can be an excellent choice for carrying an abundance of gear over the long haul. BETH PULITI

grocery shopping or staying in a hotel or hostel. It is relatively easy to access contents throughout the day, and many models are waterproof.

Cons: The weight of two racks and four panniers adds up quickly, so evaluate just how much carrying volume you will need. A single rack with two panniers can save nearly half the weight. Not all bikes are equipped with rack mounts, so you'll need to assess the compatibility of your bike with various rack options. The handling of your bike will be notably different when equipped with loaded panniers, so build in some time for test runs.

Tip: With the generous volume panniers provide, you are bound to have an abundance of items with you. Organization is key, so use color-coordinated stuff sacks to organize and differentiate contents. Getting in a routine and packing the same items in the same panniers each day will save time and hassle when searching for items on the road. Keep commonly needed items, like rain gear, snacks, and lunch, accessible on top to keep you from digging through your panniers throughout the day. Being organized is especially important when accessing items in rain and inclement weather to prevent your gear from getting wet.

Color-coded stuff sacks can help keep gear organized, particularly when you are carrying everything you need for a year or more. JUSTIN KLINE

Tip: Lower price point panniers are not always waterproof, but you can ensure your gear stays dry by lining them with garbage bags, or better yet, trash compactor bags. Once lined, pack all your items, including your sleeping bag, inside, and roll the bags from the top down several times to push the air out and make a watertight seal. This will create a fully waterproofed carrier for only a few bucks and just 2 additional ounces each.

Trailers

Bike trailers are another option for carrying gear and are preferred by some since they create minimal strain on the bike compared to a rack and panniers. A trailer allows you to keep all your gear in one place and removes easily so you can be more mobile once your destination is reached. If you have a bike that is not equipped with rack mounts, a trailer could be a viable option, but beware of the additional weight and tendency to overpack that comes with the territory.

Pros: Trailers are able to carry an abundance of gear, food, and other items, making them useful for tours with multiple people of varying strength and ability or when carrying additional gear for children. The larger profile and typically included flag create added visibility for motorists passing by.

You may commit to a lightweight carrying setup, but soon realize not everything fits, leaving you attaching items anywhere available. If you aren't a lightweight packer, a trailer could be an option for you. BETH PULITI

Cons: In addition to the obvious weight penalty, trailers can be difficult to navigate on tight trails and narrow paths. It is also more difficult for a hotel, bus, trail, or airplane to accommodate you with a trailer. The addition of a trailer also adds potential failure points—another tire and different tube size to carry, proprietary mounts, and other moving parts.

A bike trailer allows you to bring everything but the kitchen sink. In this case the Argentinian couple piloting these rigs even brought along a guitar. They were lying exhausted in the shade when we passed by. BETH PULITI

Tip: A trailer bag or box can seem like a bottomless pit. First, organize items in separate stuff sacks and then in the larger trailer bag to keep things easy to locate and dry.

Tip: Attachment pins and other proprietary mounts where the trailer connects to the frame tend to be weak points. Be sure to bring a spare hinge pin or other proprietary parts to ensure you are not left broken down without a hard-to-find part.

Backpacks/Hydration Packs

Backpacks and hydration packs have become standard equipment for many when mountain biking longer durations. They can serve as a stand-alone carrying method on shorter jaunts or be integrated into other carrying methods mentioned here. Hydration packs offer the convenience of being able to drink while on the bike and also offer additional carrying volume.

Pros: Hydration packs allow you to easily drink while riding. If carrying water in a hydration pack, the space within the bike's main triangle is freed up to accommodate a frame bag rather than water bottle cages. When everything doesn't fit on the bike, a pack is an easy way to add carrying capacity/volume to your packing system, and you'll appreciate a pack for resupplying in town, sightseeing, or during a day off the bike.

A hydration pack can be an integral part of a bikepacking or rackless touring setup.
Beth Puliti

Cons: A hydration pack/backpack adds extra weight for minimal carrying capacity, so depending upon your setup, it may not be necessary. A pack adds weight directly on the rider, which can result in strain to numerous parts of your body. In warmer weather a pack adds to your overall body heat, particularly back sweat.

Tip: A hydration pack/backpack is a great place to store accessible water and lightweight items, but don't use a backpack with too much volume. Too big of a pack will add unnecessary strain to your body and could cause loads in the open space of the pack to shift while riding. The bulk of your gear and weight should be transported on your bike. The main contents of a pack should be water, snacks, and smaller items so you don't have to regularly dig through larger panniers or frame bags.

Ultralight Carrying Methods and Why They're Right

The foundation of ultralight touring and bikepacking starts with the carrying system. Racks, panniers, trailers, and backpacks all have their place for bicycle touring, but when you are looking to cover more ground, turn the pedals over more easily, and enjoy the simplicity and freedom of a compact setup on your bike, then an ultralight bikepacking configuration, utilizing only frame bags, is the way to go.

Even extended off-road trips can be lightweight. This bikepacking setup is for a month on the Great Divide. JUSTIN KLINE

Bikepacking, as the name implies, is a harmonization of backpacking and cycling that is typically synonymous with a lightweight setup for touring, often off-road. Both ultralight touring and bikepacking are based on the principle that less is more. Carrying less weight means you can cover more ground, have less fatigue on your body and bike, and enjoy a better handling bike, which is especially important when exploring singletrack.

Frame bags are the ultimate lightweight carrying solution, and depending upon the bike, a typical setup can include a main triangle frame bag, oversized seat bag, and a large handlebar bag. By utilizing these types of bags that attach directly to your seatpost, frame, or handlebars, you will save significant weight before you even consider what to bring along.

Math Time!

Carrying System	Average Empty Weight	Weight Difference
Seat and handlebar bag	1.7 lbs.	—
Seat, frame, and bar bags	2.5 lbs.	+0.7 lb.
Rack and panniers (front and rear)	10.5 lbs.	+8.8 lbs.
Bike trailer and bag	17 lbs.	+15.3 lbs.

A seat bag designed for bikepacking and ultralight touring can be the single most useful bag in this configuration, and is much different than the traditional under-the-saddle tool bag that most cyclists are accustomed to. It provides a single, easy-to-access, large-volume space that can house a variety of gear. For day trips and shorter excursions, a seat bag can be used as a stand-alone carrying system. For longer trips it can be used to carry a wide variety of gear, and can often be used to attach additional items on top or below as well.

A bikepacking seat bag, such as the Viscacha from Revelate Designs, is a staple for a lightweight bikepacking setup. REVELATE DESIGNS

Tour Divide Turmoil

A number of years back while participating in Tour Divide, a self-supported off-road race from Canada to Mexico, I was plagued with a slipping seatpost. It became clear after several hundred miles that my stock seat bolt clamp was not up to the task of holding my weight along with a hydration pack and the additional weight of a loaded bikepacking seat bag. Continued slipping led to continuous tightening, but eventually I cranked down one too many revolutions and stripped the threads. A minor inconvenience under most circumstances, but in rural Montana with no bike shop for countless miles and few services beyond a café, general store, and post office, it became a much more difficult dilemma to solve. After numerous dead-end inquiries, I was fortunate to stumble upon a handyman working in his home garage re-welding an ATV frame. After coming to terms with what I was attempting to do, he kindly went to work with a tap and die, and resolved my situation with a larger replacement bolt and new threads.

—Justin Kline

Tip: A loaded seat bag can add considerable weight to your saddle and seatpost. Ensure your saddle rail bolts and seatpost bolts are securely tightened to specification to avoid slipping. On longer trips, occasional retightening may be necessary, so it is wise to carry an additional bolt for each in case one becomes stripped.

Bikepacking handlebar bags greatly differ from the traditional design of a flip-top handlebar bag typically associated with rack and pannier touring. A bikepacking handlebar bag is usually a long, cylinder-shaped (dry) bag that attaches directly to the handlebars without an additional mount. This saves weight and maximizes volume. It provides a surprising amount of storage space on an otherwise underutilized space on the bike, and has minimal impact on handling since the weight is fairly snug to the handlebars. Bikepacking handlebar bags are ideally configured on mountain bikes, where their full volume can be utilized. With drop bars on road and cyclocross bikes, the volume of a bar bag is limited due to the narrow space available between the drops, but it still provides a lightweight option for carrying items on the front of the bike

Tip: Bikepacking handlebar bags are often narrow, making them tricky to get into and out of, so organization is key. This storage space is best used for items

that are not needed while on the bike during the day, such as your sleeping kit. Depending upon your gear, you may be able to fit your entire sleep system—pad, bag, and shelter—in the handlebar bag. Tent poles are ideally stored by strapping them on the underside of the handlebar bag.

Frame bags, designed to mount within the main triangle of your bike, are an excellent place to store a variety of items, especially if they are heavy. Items stored within a main triangle frame bag keep the weight centered with a relatively lower center of gravity, allowing your bike to handle better than with weight carried in alternative locations. A main triangle frame bag does cover your bottle cage mounts, so you can either create two small holes

A bikepacking handlebar bag transforms the underside of your handlebars into a versatile carrying space for an abundance of gear—often your sleeping system. REVELATE DESIGNS

to mount cages within the bag (assuming the other contents are well organized), or you can store a hydration bladder within the frame bag and have the hose running out to your top tube for convenient access.

Tip: Most frame bags are designed to fit specific bike manufacturer's frames and models. If your bike is not on that short list, don't worry, there are a number of custom frame bag manufacturers. You can also search online for the geometry of bikes that have available frame bags, then compare it to that of your own bike. Often there's an available size and configuration that will fit the bill.

Here is a list of some of the leading frame bag manufacturers:

- Revelate Designs   revelatedesigns.com
- Porcelain Rocket   porcelainrocket.com
- Bedrock Bags   bedrockbags.com
- Wanderlust Gear   wanderlust-gear.com
- Oveja Negra Threadworks   ovejanegrathreadworks.com

These manufacturers offer handlebar bags, frame bags (some both custom and stock), seat bags, and a variety of other carry bags for the fork legs,

Frame bags can be custom-made to perfectly fit your frame, and can include multiple compartments and other features depending upon your needs. REVELATE DESIGNS

top tube, and just about everywhere else you can cram carrying space onto your bike.

Committing to a lightweight carrying system ensures you start your journey on the right weight-saving foot from the start. Not only will a frame bag configuration save you significant weight in itself, but also the nature of such a packing system promotes saving ounces and pounds throughout.

Less space to fill (within frame bags compared to panniers and trailers) means you will naturally bring less weight, or downsize the equipment you do bring. It's human nature that if there is extra space available, we are going to fill it with something that we might need or that would be nice to have just in case. The nice thing about using a frame bag setup for touring and backpacking is that it limits weight and the ability to overpack right from the start, because there isn't an abundance of space available for those "maybe" items.

A lighter carrying system and load also allows you to use a lighter bike and lighter wheels. Traditional touring bikes rely on overbuilt steel frames and

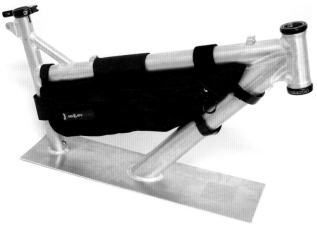

Most frame bag manufacturers offer stock bags to fit a variety of locations on the bike. This stock small frame bag is one such option that also allows you to use your water bottle cages. REVELATE DESIGNS

Even winter trips can be ultralight with a bikepacking setup. Justin Kline

heavy-duty wheels to deal with the added load they typically carry. While they are great at this task and extremely durable, this durability is again added weight that can easily be shed if you are committed to a bikepacking or ultralight system. With a bikepacking carrying system, you can forgo purpose-built touring and cargo bikes and use lightweight frame material options, such as carbon fiber instead of steel. The weight savings ultimately becomes exponential.

Beyond the cumulative weight-saving possibilities, an ultralight load also means a more enjoyable ride. For some that means the ability to cover more miles per day, and for others it is about more time to enjoy the destination at the end of the day. Whatever the motive, we can all agree that a light and compact load is easier to bring along as you pedal throughout the day.

No single carrying method is right for every situation. Depending upon the type of riding you are doing, the destination, and the duration of the ride, there may be clear advantages to one or more of the carrying methods discussed. More often than not, limiting your load and streamlining your setup will prove most enjoyable, but always take all the details of your trip into account, many of which can be determined when planning your tour.

CHAPTER THREE

Trip Planning and Logistics

Planning a bike tour can be nearly as exciting as the adventure itself—reviewing your gear, plotting your course, and taking a glimpse into the unknown journey that lies ahead. With any trip to a new destination, there are bound to be unknown elements, but don't fret over these details. As long as you are prepared, everything else will fall into place.

Your tour plans might not call for cave exploration, but why not stop and indulge? BETH PULITI

37

Bike touring and bikepacking mean traveling at a slower pace than daily rides. Be sure to budget time to stop and enjoy the scenery, as it changes around every bend. BETH PULITI

The amount of research required during the planning phase of a tour will depend on your comfort level and inclination to wing it on the road. A short overnight journey or weekend trip can be executed on a whim; a weeklong or longer excursion should be prefaced with at least a few hours of planning, and a yearlong international adventure often takes several months to a year or more of research and planning.

The best piece of advice when it comes to trip preparation: Don't over-plan. Ensuring you are well prepared with gear is of course important, but you will find bike touring, like most adventures, is best enjoyed when it evolves naturally during the course of the journey. On longer trips, having rigid nightly destinations and timelines can add stress and take away from the natural progression. Often you will find the best recommendations come from locals along the way. Their knowledge can go a long way in shaping the perfect tour. Going with the flow is not for everyone, though. If you are prone to fear of the unknown while traveling, then a guided tour may be another option to consider.

Before the dots on the map become miles on your odometer, one of the first important decisions to make is whether your tour will be a solo adventure or with a partner or group of friends. This decision usually comes down to the type of person you are and your demeanor in general. Here are some considerations to help you make the decision:

* Do you prefer alone time?

* How well do you know your potential touring partner(s)?

- Do you both ride at a similar pace when cycling?
- Are you comfortable sharing accommodations?
- Do you have sufficient gear to travel solo or would sharing better suit you?
- Are you capable and confident to navigate on your own?
- Do you and your potential touring partner(s) have similar touring experience and traveling styles?
- Do you both prefer to camp or stay in hotels?
- Are you or someone in the group capable of basic bicycle maintenance?
- Are you and your potential touring partner(s) capable of covering the proposed route within the allotted time frame?
- Are you self-sufficient when it comes to accommodations, camping, and meal preparation? If not, a guided tour might be more suitable.

Once you have established your trip as a solo endeavor or an outing with a partner(s), it is a good idea to review the proposed route. Plotting a route often involves setting an average daily mileage total to determine the duration of the

Touring or bikepacking with a group of close friends can be an unforgettable experience. It was all smiles for our group during this weekend outing in the White Mountains of New Hampshire. Beth Puliti

Up, up, and away. Some days it can feel like you are climbing forever. Be sure to take elevation change into account when estimating daily mileage. BETH PULITI

trip. There are many variables that affect daily mileage estimates, so take into account the following factors before making daily distance assumptions:

- Your traveling speed while touring will be notably slower than your regular cycling speed due to the added weight of your gear
- Allow ample time for taking in the sights, meeting new people, and exploring along the way
- Elevation gain/loss on the route
- Prevailing winds
- Time for regular food, water, and bathroom breaks
- The more people in your group, the longer everything takes—eating, setting up camp, breaking down, etc.

For planning long journeys, across several countries for example, 50 kilometers (31 miles) a day is often a good baseline estimate for a bike tour that can last a month or more. This casual estimate allows time for sightseeing and days off, and time to enjoy new destinations.

Since transportation systems in most parts of the world are built around traveling by car, getting from point A to point B following the shortest route is seldom the best option when bike touring. It is best to reference a number of resources when plotting your course at home, including:

- Google Maps—a convenient starting point to determine mileage; use their bike option to identify less traveled roads.

- Scribble Maps—a good resource to draw potential routes onto a Google Map so you can save, print, or upload them to a smartphone for use later.

- Adventure Cycling Association (adventurecycling.org)—an excellent resource for touring routes and additional resources specific to traveling by bike.

- Local rail trail associations and other dedicated touring organizations—provide electronic and paper maps for sale and also offer an abundance of trip planning resources.

- Cycling-specific mapping and fitness sites like Strava, Bikely, and Mapmyride—offer a glimpse of rides fellow cyclists have taken, along with comments, which can provide a baseline for identifying suitable routes when roads on the map are foreign to you.

Ride Local

While exploring faraway destinations by bike can be enticing, don't be afraid to ride out your front door and explore what your local area has to offer. The slower speed of traveling by bike allows you to see things in a whole new way, and often you find new roads and discover new sights that are commonly overlooked by those in automobiles.

Even the local hills you are accustomed to driving will feel far different when experienced on your loaded bike. Justin Kline

One great way to explore locally, and on a regular basis, is by taking an S24H trip, or sub-24-hour excursion. This term was coined by Grant Peterson, founder of Rivendell Bicycle Works, Walnut Creek, California, for taking short (less than 24 hours) overnight journeys by bike. It is especially great for people with families and small children who cannot venture out for long. Pedal out the front door in the afternoon, ride to a nearby destination to spend the night, and ride home the next day.

Adventure Cycling now has a site that encourages the sharing of routes and stories—bikeovernights.com. There you'll find a number of S24H trips as well as longer journeys organized by state to inspire you and aid in planning for upcoming tours of your own.

Exploring the local New England snowmobile trails with good friends. BETH PULITI

CHAPTER FOUR

Hitting the Road

If you are not accustomed to traveling by bicycle with only the supplies you can carry, the scenario might seem a bit daunting at first, but the experience is far from that. You might be thinking: What do I eat? Where do I find water? Where do I sleep? Where do I shower and clean my clothes? How do I navigate? All are valid questions, but don't be intimidated. There are multiple answers to such questions, and all are part of the joy of exploring by bike. When forced to focus on the simple tasks of everyday living, you learn to maintain a simple lifestyle free of the worries associated with a work-centric lifestyle that most people live.

What to Eat

One of the joys of bike touring is the amount of food it allows you to consume. A full day on the bike can burn 10,000-plus calories. That means plenty of snack breaks throughout the day to keep you energized (and to take a

Heading out to explore by bike is exhilarating. See how exciting it is! BETH PULITI

Fresh fruit found roadside along the way makes for excellent snacks. BETH PULITI

break from turning over the pedals). At the end of a full day in the saddle, you are likely to still be left feeling empty and ready to replenish with a full meal. Depending upon your preference and accommodations, you may be able to cook your meals, purchase premade foods in delis or supermarkets, or in some cases find freshly made street food, along your route. Here are some guidelines and go-to options on the road:

Breakfast

Oatmeal

Granola and powdered milk

Doughnuts

Pastries

Toast with jam

Fresh fruit

Snack crackers

Coffee or tea

Sometimes your hunger can't wait until the next town. This curve in Croatia did just fine for filling my stomach. BETH PULITI

Just some of the many choices for keeping your energy level up while riding all day long. JUSTIN KLINE

Lunch/Snacks

Dried fruits
Energy bars
Sandwiches
Wraps
Peanut butter
Hard cheeses
Beef jerky
Trail mix
Tuna packets
Pizza

Nuts provide excellent nutrition while on the road. You might be lucky enough to receive them as a gift from a passing stranger, as we did in rural Turkey. BETH PULITI

Dinner

When your day on the bike ends with a campsite—wild or organized—a hot meal over a campfire or portable camp stove is a rewarding finish. Dehydrated camping meals are convenient and available in a variety of creative combinations. For less-expensive options, dehydrated soups, instant mashed potatoes, pasta, and other shelf-stable, just-add-water foods can be cooked with minimal effort.

Not all dining locations are created equally. Why not dine with a view? BETH PULITI

If spending the night in a hotel, you'll typically have the luxury of a cooked meal on the premises, or there will likely be an eating establishment nearby. The use of camping stoves in hotels is always prohibited, but if you want to prepare your own meal, look for a room with a balcony or ground-floor private entrance.

Sometimes after a long day in the saddle, there isn't a restaurant in sight and the prospect of cooking is too overwhelming. In these scenarios pre-made sandwiches, jerky, cheese and crackers, and canned goods make for convenient no-cook dinners at the end of the day.

While you may be traveling with a limited spice cabinet, you'll find you can prepare a delicious meal almost anywhere, like this olive grove in Turkey. BETH PULITI

Variety Is the Spice of Life

I once embarked on a 420-mile self-supported (and navigated) race
across the state of Pennsylvania. The no-entry-fee, no-waiver, limited-
rules nature of the event attracts a variety of competitors, from local
bike messengers to randonneurs (unsupported endurance cyclists)
to casual riders, making for an entertaining ensemble of cyclists.
About 200 or so miles into the event, I came across a first-time partici-
pant running a pretty traditional touring setup, although a bit heavy
given the length of the event. After coming out of the local mini-mart,
we began to chat, since he was in awe of the caloric-laden fast-food
meal and snacks I was about to consume. He confessed that for nutrition he was carrying nothing but a single flavor of energy bar to fuel
him for however long it would take to cycle the 420-mile route, which
explained his abnormally surprised reaction to my local cuisine on
the go. He had apparently calculated the number of energy bars
he normally consumed on a 20-mile ride, multiplied that by 21, and
arrived at a pannier full of chocolate-flavored PowerBars. Unless you
are looking for a reason to go on a hunger strike, I would suggest not
following such a calculation. —Justin Kline

Whichever method you prefer, cooking or buying prepared food, be aware
of your energy expenditure and calorie consumption to ensure your body is
getting enough nutrition to sustain the repeated exertion day after day.

Where to Get Water

Drinking plenty of water while touring by bike is an obvious necessity, especially in the heat of the summer. The amount you should consume (sometimes
the amount you need is far more than you think) and where to find it will vary.

When road touring in the United States, safe drinking water is seldom
difficult to find. Tap water, bottled water, and natural sources are all viable
options (be sure to treat when collecting water from an unknown natural
source; see details on water filtering in chapter 8). Learn to look for water in
new places and find alternatives, such as garden hoses, and within public
buildings at parks, churches, and schools.

In addition to plain old water, many cyclists use electrolyte drinks and
supplements during rides and tours. These can help replenish vitamins and
minerals lost through sweat. Rather than carry the weight of ready-made

electrolyte drinks, the best option for touring is to bring it along in the readily available concentrated powder form, which allows you to easily mix it in your bike bottles. You can alternate between straight water and mix as needed, and also alternate flavors.

Dehydration is no joke. Despite drinking nearly a gallon of water the day before, I ended up in the emergency room in Croatia for dehydration and heat exhaustion the next morning. BETH PULITI

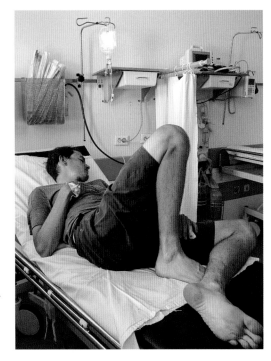

Water can be found from a variety of sources, including fountains. Be sure water is potable or filter it before consuming. BETH PULITI

Where to Sleep

Spending the night outside your normal walls and at a destination reached by your own power makes for a fulfilling day and a good night's rest. Where you lay your head may be dictated by the surroundings, but in general your choices are camping or staying in accommodations.

Wild Camping

Wild camping—camping outside of designated camping facilities—is notably different from backpacking since cyclists are often traveling on roads rather than trails. Because of this, finding camp spots on private or open space land is often more involved when bike touring compared to backpacking or off-road bikepacking.

If you are looking to spend most of your overnight time wild camping, then timing is of the utmost importance. A routine of wild camping when road or gravel touring means your goal each day is to seek out a camp spot in the golden hour before sunset, and break down your campsite in the morning hour surrounding sunrise. Working within this window keeps you mostly invisible from curious onlookers and helps ensure you can get a good night's rest without worry. Allow an hour or so before dark at the end of the day to find a suitable wild camp spot; it gets more difficult to find a good spot after dark.

There is no better feeling than ending the day at a remote campsite under the stars.
Beth Puliti

Quick Guide to Campsite Selection

Depending on where you're touring, you may have to camp in specific locations because of local rules, but in many areas you may choose to camp wherever you want. Here are some guidelines for finding a good camping spot when options abound.

Three-season camping: Many impacted campsites will be found along rivers and lakes, in saddles, and in other flat areas. These are often great places to camp because they've been established, and you won't be impacting a new site. They're often easy to set up on and flat.

Try not to set up camp in fragile areas like meadows, on fragile vegetation, or too close to a water source, especially if they are limited, such as in a desert, because you can greatly impact the habits of wildlife.

Camping near bodies of water is nice because it's often scenic, and

Besides making for a fitful night sleeping, this is the nightmare you wake up to in a bad campsite when it is raining heavily—sleeping in a puddle and everything soaking wet. JUSTIN LICHTER

you don't need to carry water to cook with, but cold air settles around lakes and low points, which can make it colder than camping in a forest. Air near a water source is also moist, so you're likely to have more condensation form on your shelter or sleeping bag when camping nearby. We're not the only ones attracted to water, so you're likely to find more unwelcome bugs around water too. If bugs are an issue, camp out in the open and away from water, perhaps where there might be a breeze like on a ridgeline or in a saddle. You can also—if it's safe—start a small smoke fire to try to get rid of them.

When you'll be sleeping in the next morning or setting up a multiday base camp, try to set up in a shady spot. It keeps your tent cooler and, by avoiding UV radiation, helps the fabrics last longer.

Try to find a spot that is sheltered from the wind if bugs aren't an issue. When that's not an option, face the narrow part of your tent or shelter into the wind. This will reduce wind noise and the chances that the shelter will be broadsided by wind, which can otherwise keep you up all night.

Try not to set up camp where the ground is compacted, since these are places where water might run off and pool under your shelter if it rains overnight. This is even more important when sleeping in a canyon—make sure you're not set up in a spot that could get hit by a flash flood. If you think it may rain or flash flood, make sure you have an exit route prepared.

When camping on a beach, camp well above the high-tide line.

When camping on a previously undisturbed spot, try to minimize your impact by putting natural items (rocks, branches, pine needles, etc.) back where you found them. Leave the site just as you found it by making it look like no one camped there. That minimizes the chance that someone else will see it and use the spot as a campsite, resulting in another impacted area.

When looking for a good campsite, think about possible dangers including people, weather, and animals. Animals can easily, though usually accidentally, rip your shelter. Justin Lichter

In desert areas, sandy washes make great camping areas when there's little chance of rain. They drain well, are really comfortable for sleeping, and are very low impact because nothing grows in the wash and your tracks disappear quickly.

Tip: When there's little chance of rain, sleeping under the stars (cowboy camping) can be an option too. Just throw out your groundsheet, sleeping pad, and sleeping bag and fall asleep under the starry canopy. It's easier and faster to pack up in the morning, and your otherwise unused shelter makes a nice pillow too! If it's cold and pushing the temperature range of your sleep system, then set up your shelter, since that will add 5 to 10 degrees of warmth to your sleep system.

Tip: Cold air sinks at night. To stay warmer, try not to camp in valley floors and low spots, where cold air accumulates.

Wild camping sometimes requires the stealth cover of vegetation. BETH PULITI

Tips for Wild Camping

Don't force it. If you are not comfortable with a wild camp spot, don't be afraid to move farther down the road or trail to find another. If you are worried about being hassled over your spot, then you'll likely be tossing and turning while your mind is running, rather than getting a good night's rest.

Ensure that your cycling clothes and gear are out of sight. Remember, cycling-specific clothing and gear, including your panniers and certain parts of your bike, are designed to be highly visible to motorists and lights. If you are camping near a road or trail, you should ensure all cycling gear is out of the path of potential headlights of vehicles passing by.

Ideal camp locations include farm fields, churches, and mountainside switchbacks. Just remember that if a landowner is present, it is always best to ask for permission in advance. Chances are you will be happily hosted on their plot of land for the evening.

Take note of the surrounding foliage. Rolling into the bushes at dusk can make unwanted hazards like thorns and poison ivy difficult to see. The last thing you want is to wake up with flat tires and uncontrollable itching.

If you are on BLM or US Forest Service land, camping anywhere, unless otherwise signed, is completely legal and free.

Campgrounds

Organized campgrounds can be wonderful places to lay your head for the night after a day of riding. Typically, organized campgrounds are easily found on maps, making for simple navigation and ideal end-of-the-day destinations. Campgrounds can be either privately run operations or government run in state parks or other wilderness areas. Both can be enjoyable ways to end the day of riding, but have advantages and disadvantages depending upon how you plan to spend your evening.

Private campgrounds:
Can be expensive
Often offer more services and luxuries
Sometimes have a restaurant on-site or nearby

State park/government campgrounds:
Sometimes do not allow alcohol
Can require using an advance reservation system
Can allow only tent camping for a more rural experience

Tips for organized campgrounds: Campground facilities mean you can often travel lighter by carrying less gear. If your campsite permits fires and is equipped with a ring/grill, then leave the camp stove behind. Washroom and shower facilities also allow you to carry a smaller toiletry kit, and in some cases less clothing.

Organized campgrounds, especially private operations, often cater to recreational vehicles as well. Be sure to seek out a site clear of the RV section of the campground to avoid potentially hearing generators all night.

Hotels

A long day in the saddle followed by sleeping outside is not for everyone; for some a hotel, inn, bed-and-breakfast, or other such accommodation provides closure, comfort, and security at the end of a long day on the bike. Hotel hopping by bike allows you to ditch the weight of a tent and other gear, to travel more freely, and enjoy comforts at the end of each day. This of course comes with an added daily expense. Even if you are a diehard camper, however, a hotel can provide the occasional respite needed from the elements and a chance to recharge the batteries, figuratively and literally.

Here are some advantages to the occasional hotel stay while traveling:

- Shower and a chance to clean up

- Internet access

- Opportunity to do laundry

- Comfortable night's sleep

- Out of the elements

- Security of your bike and gear (assuming it is allowed to join you in the room)

- Opportunity to recharge devices, watch TV, and relax

It doesn't take a fancy hotel to make you appreciate luxury. Even after just a few days on the road, the comforts of a hotel are much appreciated. Wi-fi lures those of us working from the road with the need to reconnect. BETH PULITI

On the road you learn to sleep wherever you can—in this case while transiting on an overnight ferry from Greece to Turkey. BETH PULITI

Alternative Lodging Options

The Internet has allowed for a new type of lodging option to evolve as well. Now with websites and apps like Warmshowers and Couchsurfing, you can reach out to a local host in advance. Not only does this form of lodging save you the hotel expense for a night, but it can also be an excellent way to meet new people and learn about the destination and the surrounding area.

Warmshowers has been an indispensable resource while touring in other parts of the world. The experience of meeting a stranger who shares the common love of cycling and welcomes you into their home is, in most cases, an unforgettable experience. It provides an opportunity to meet new people, gain valuable local insight, and sometimes share a home-cooked meal together.

Couchsurfing relies on similar principles as Warmshowers, but without the bike touring common bond. Your potential host or guest could be a bit more random and lack a common interest or similar personality. What is nice about Couchsurfing, though, is that this general approach offers an abundance of lodging opportunities worldwide, particularly in locations where Warmshowers hosts may not be present or are already occupied with another guest.

How to Stay Clean

When the majority of your day is spent pedaling, it doesn't take long before you and your limited wardrobe are covered in sweat and grime. Reserving and changing into an off-the-bike outfit at the end of the day brings a comforting and "almost clean" feeling, but nothing beats a warm shower beforehand. If you are not staying in an organized campground or hotel, you may be wondering: How does one come by such a cleansing? Luckily there are a number of alternative options:

Lakes and rivers—A refreshing swim and cleansing bath, all at once. Just remember to never use soap products directly in or near bodies of water.

Portable shower—There are a number of camp showers on the market; unfortunately, most are bulky and targeted to car campers. The exception is the Sea to Summit Pocket Shower—a worthy piece of gear if you feel the need for a daily shower while wild camping.

Baby wipes—When a real shower is not an option, baby wipes are the next best thing. Carrying a small pack can keep you clean for several days in between real showers. This is a convenient option when wild camping with hotel access on a weekly basis.

Bathhouse or locker room—Depending on where your travels take you, a public bathhouse or fee shower may be an option. The YMCA, gyms, sporting complexes, and truck stops are just a few of the options for finding an elusive shower on the road. Even if not advertised as a stand-alone service, it never hurts to ask how much it costs for a shower. In many cases the attendant will likely offer it for free.

If you are traveling by bike for more than a few days, laundry is another consideration if you want to keep from scaring away the locals. As with showering this is another service much easier to come by at hotels and organized campgrounds. Don't feel obligated to pay for overpriced laundry services though. In your bathroom sink you can make short work of two pairs of bike shorts, socks, and a shirt or two. When wild camping, laundry can be a bit trickier. With merino wool, dipping and wringing the shirt out usually gets the bulk of the sweat and grime out. You can also pack something like the collapsible Granite Gear Kitchen Sink for laundry and dishes. As a bonus it can also be filled up with water and used for locating those hard-to-find holes in your tubes, water bladder, or sleeping pad.

Tip: Laundry detergent can be hard to come by in small doses. If you can't find a single-load portion, body wash or shampoo does the trick just fine with hot water.

Tip: If your garments did not dry overnight, let the sun and wind finish the job while you are riding. Your rack is the perfect place to air out your latest laundry load. Clothes are then easily accessible to hang dry or lay out when you stop for a break or lunch.

After washing your bike clothes in the hotel room sink, it's time to let them air dry. BETH PULITI

How to Navigate

Once your course has been set, you'll need to ensure you are able to navigate your route while on the bike. For some, the luxury of a GPS unit producing turn-by-turn directions is desirable, but it is much easier than you think to navigate by map, either paper or digital.

When navigating by a digital map, presumably on your phone, consider the following:

- Uses an excess of cellular data if constantly referencing your location and navigating directions (this can be disabled)

- Allows you to easily find your current location

- Relies on battery power that can run out and leave you lost

- Requires a waterproof case for navigation in inclement weather

- Often has limited viewing of off-road routes and trails

    When navigating by paper map, consider the following:

- Look for a scale between 1:200,000 to 1:500,000 to provide adequate detail of terrain and road infrastructure, without getting into too much unnecessary detail and needing too many maps each day

- Can be cumbersome when covering large areas

- Always accessible without battery power

- Sometimes unreliable in foreign countries or not up to date (new logging roads or jeep roads have popped up)

- Requires carrying a compass to ensure you can identify your location and course

- Statewide and larger-scale maps can lack the detail required to navigate cities by bike

    Should a GPS unit be your preferred method of navigation, here are a few things to keep in mind:

- Do you have a power source to recharge the GPS when necessary, or will you get to town often enough to recharge?

- Do the available maps cover your proposed route? This is especially important when traveling off-road.

- Can you easily remove the unit from your bike when necessary?

- If it is stormy, cloudy, or tree-covered, do you feel comfortable navigating without the GPS if the GPS is taking a long time to lock onto satellites?

CHAPTER FIVE

International Considerations

Exploring outside your own country is undoubtedly an adventure no matter what the circumstances, but when the avenue for exploration is by bicycle the world becomes an even more exciting experience. Touring on international soil presents a number of new challenges and a variety of factors to keep in mind.

Transporting Your Bike

Unless you are traveling with a folding bike or travel bike designed to fit within an airline-approved-size suitcase, you'll likely have an additional transportation expense for your bike to take into account.

When departing from the United States, cardboard bike boxes are typically easy to come by. When returning home from a foreign country, they can be more difficult to find. After reading the airline regulations, you may be able to get away with securing the handlebars, removing the pedals, and wrapping the bike as shown. BETH PULITI

Shipping via UPS, FedEx, or other international carrier is an option, but despite rising airline costs, bringing your bike on the airplane is still typically more economical. With more flight options from budget foreign airlines, it is worth investigating their baggage policy and comparing it to other fares. Some foreign carriers charge baggage solely based on weight, which can save you $150 or more each way on bike handling fees assessed by US-based carriers.

Packing Your Bike

It is nearly impossible to keep up with constantly changing airline regulations and fees these days, so it's important to read your airline's specific policy on baggage and the handling of bicycles prior to packing. In general, though, you should have about 23 kilograms (50 pounds) to work with, but this can vary depending upon whether it is a US- or foreign-based airline. Size restrictions will vary, but using a cardboard bike box from your local bike shop should put you within the allotted dimensions. Once your bike is packed securely (by yourself or the local shop), you can use the surrounding space to pack a good amount of your touring kit. Ideally, you should be able to fit most of your equipment in with the bike and leave either your panniers or frame bags to carry onboard with the remaining items. Running tubeless tires? Although all airlines say you need to deflate the tires, you can simply let a little out, but keep sufficient pressure to allow your tubeless bead seal to remain intact.

International Payment

Purchasing goods and services outside of the country will of course require using the currency of the local destination, and it is helpful to have some advance knowledge of the local currency. Here are a few things to keep an eye on before arriving at your foreign destination:

- Research the current exchange rate compared to your native currency (or that of the neighboring country when cycling across borders).

- Determine if credit cards or debit cards are commonly accepted. This will dictate how much cash you will need to exchange, withdraw, and carry around with you.

- A quick search of accommodations and food costs in advance will help determine the amount of currency you'll need as well.

Obtaining currency in foreign countries is typically carried out by either withdrawing money from a local ATM, or bringing US currency to exchange at a local bank or currency exchange service. If you are planning to draw from your US bank account or make purchases with your debit card, double-check that your bank does not charge additional international transaction fees (typically 1 to 3 percent).

Tip: I suggest a credit or debit card like the CapitalOne card or Charles Schwab Platinum debit card that does not charge an international service charge and is accommodating for a variety of services while traveling abroad. You can also accumulate points for rewards with your purchases.

Tip: When exchanging a larger sum of money in developed countries, avoid exchanging upon arrival at airports and other port destinations, which typically offer an unfavorable rate compared to a local bank or even an ATM.

Not all credit cards are created equally, and neither is their acceptance outside of the United States. In foreign countries that actually accept credit cards for payment, many will require one with a chip in it. Although cards with chips are slowly becoming more common in the United States, if you don't have one, it may behoove you to sign up for an alternative credit card with a chip in advance of your foreign travels. Just be sure there are no foreign transaction fees associated with the card. You will quickly find that numerous amenities and services abroad cannot be paid for by credit card, particularly in less-developed nations. In most of the Balkans and Southeast Asia, for example, you'll primarily be paying for hotels and other accommodations in cash.

Established Route Systems

Just as we have the Adventure Cycling Association in the United States, some foreign countries have established route networks that make touring abroad a simplified endeavor. One great example of this is the Euro Velo route system in Europe. The current network of fourteen routes offers more than 70,000 kilometers of mapped routes throughout Europe, with the number of routes and total distance still growing annually. Established networks such as the Euro Velo system can provide an abundance of touring options with minimal research and fear of the unknown. Don't be afraid to venture on roads outside of suggested touring routes, as these often provide the most rewarding experiences in terms of interaction with locals who are less likely to see bike travelers passing through their villages.

Navigation

Unlike the United States, road signs in many countries do not indicate direction, even on major routes. We are accustomed to seeing signs like I-95 North,

Knowing the town names along your daily route can save time fussing with maps when touring abroad. BETH PULITI

which you will be hard-pressed to find abroad. Unless you are overly confident in your navigation skills, it is best to familiarize yourself with towns along your route, and even in the opposite direction, to ensure you are headed in the right direction even on primary roads. While touring abroad, offline mapping software can be really helpful to get around. There's no paper map clutter and it offers details not often found on generic paper maps, such as identifying lodging, food options, and banks. Currently an offline mapping app called Maps.Me has some handy features. Electronic maps are particularly valuable in cities where a higher level of detail is required to navigate the expanse of road options and attempt to differentiate between freeways and lower traffic roadways. Simply download the map of your country in advance and (depending upon your mobile phone) you'll be able to view your current location on the map and use it as you navigate, free of data roaming and other charges.

Tip: To limit the amount of time you need to fumble over a map, start your day with a list of towns along your route—that way you can rely on road signs to find your way.

Tip: Adjust the unit of measurement on your cycling computer to kilometers to correlate with foreign road signs and maps.

Tip: When you are looking for clarification on directions to your destination, do not simply point in a direction and ask if it goes to your desired town. You'll likely receive a head nod or a "yes" every time from someone who does not fully understand what you are asking. Instead, to help clarify your where-abouts, point in the specific direction and ask where the road or trail goes to, or make sure to ask non-leading questions.

Road Conditions

Outside the United States you'll find the condition of roads varies greatly, from the pristine motorways and separate bike paths in Germany, to the pothole-ridden roadways in the Balkans, to the forgotten dirt and gravel paths of Southeast Asia. In general you should consider a larger-volume tire than you typically ride to accommodate for varied surfaces and rougher terrain. Such road conditions also require special attention to situations we typically take for granted in the United States. Missing manhole covers, roadsides that give way to significant dropoffs, and storm grates with oversized openings between bars are all common obstructions abroad, which can lead to incidents ending your trip or landing you in the hospital.

Pavement ends and shoulders drop off without warning. This can be a common scene, even on regularly traveled roads, outside of the United States. Beth Puliti

Riding Highways

Chances are most of your planned rides at home don't include stints along the side of the interstate, but depending on your touring destination and route outside the country, sections of highway riding may be unavoidable. In due time it is not uncommon to find a local on a recreational ride or a routine local traveler along the same busy road, a surreal but somehow comforting feeling in this situation. You should, however, be aware that in many countries cycling on the highway is illegal. Research the regulations on your route beforehand.

The reliability of road signage overseas varies, as seen here in Macedonia. BETH PULITI

Sometimes a dilapidated sidewalk is the safe place to ride. When entering Athens, we had some stretches of sidewalk and others of shoulder-less highway. BETH PULITI

Be prepared to mingle amid other modes of transportation abroad. In some places almost anything goes when it comes to driving age, safety laws, and luggage transporting. All part of the adventure! BETH PULITI

International Drivers

Driving habits, laws, and circumstances tend to vary outside the United States as well. In some countries drunk driving is still a common problem and seldom enforced. In parts of Greece and some countries in Africa, you may encounter what appears to be a shoulder equal to the width of the primary lane of travel; most trucks and slower vehicles travel the "shoulder." As someone accustomed to the US transportation system, you are likely to find most cities abroad to feel notably more chaotic. Take some time to observe the driving habits and customs of the city, and don't be afraid to integrate into their system. In many cases priority is given to those who grant it upon themselves, whether that is a truck, taxi, scooter, or pedestrian. Don't be afraid to hold your ground and safely make your presence on the bike known. This can be done safely and effectively without causing confrontation or dangerous encounters, since traffic flow in foreign urban environments is usually built around anticipating the movement of others.

Honking

If you are a cyclist from the United States, you, like most cyclists, likely cringe when a passing motorist sounds their horn on your behalf. The majority of motorists in this country are honking to alert you of their presence or to highlight their elevated annoyance with your presence on the road. Outside the United States, honking is far more common, but fortunately, not typically used by drivers as an aggressive gesture. In many countries drivers honk to cheer you on, support your efforts, and let you know they genuinely appreciate you visiting their country. Albania takes the crown for most zealous drivers!

Scooters

Outside the United States the far side of the white line is often used by more than bicycles. Motorized scooters can make up a majority of the traffic occupying the space outside the primary lanes of travel. As a touring cyclist in Southeast Asia, for instance, you are bound to be the minority traveling on two wheels without a motor. While this is worth noting, don't let the zooming scooters intimidate you. Most are considerate drivers and excited to see you visiting their country.

In places like Southeast Asia, you'll find that scooters rule the shoulder, not bicycles. They'll mostly be zooming by you, but occasionally you'll be making the pass. BETH PULITI

A little research can help you fit in with local cultures. Your cycling attire may be far too revealing compared to local customs. BETH PULITI

Cultural Influences

While the mystery of the unknown is an allure for all of us, knowing a little bit about the culture of your destination in advance can go a long way. What is acceptable to wear according to your gender? What gestures, body language, and interactions are considered appropriate? Is there a religious day of rest? Is there an appropriate way to greet somebody? The diverse cultures abroad can be one of the most fascinating elements of international bike travel, so be sure to embrace it.

Restroom Differences

It may sound strange, but even something as simple as using the bathroom can be a completely unique experience outside of the United States. In some countries, such as Greece, where their plumbing systems are antiquated, toilet paper cannot be flushed and is instead deposited into waste bins within the bathroom. In other parts of the world, such as Southeast Asia, you'll likely find a "squatty potty" or "long drop loo"—something resembling a hole in the ground compared to the Western sit toilet.

The restroom scene can be a bit different than what you are used to stateside, as shown here in Thailand. BETH PULITI

Here we are strategically avoiding the hustle and bustle of Bangkok Central Station after arriving on an overnight sleeper car. Beth Puliti

Train Stations

Train stations can be a gold mine destination for a touring cyclist. As a transportation hub in many foreign communities, railway stations often offer an abundance of services depending upon their size, including restaurants, takeout food, water, restrooms, Internet access, bathrooms, showers, and sometimes even outside food vendors and markets. The stations themselves are not the only resource either; hopping on a train with your bike is an excellent way to navigate in and out of congested cities, or cover long stretches of ground quickly if need be.

Churches

Churches can be a great place of refuge when traveling abroad. In some foreign countries they can provide not only shelter but also water, a restroom, and in certain cases even lodging. You should of course be sure to respect every aspect of the religious institution and seek permission prior to using the

This church in rural Italy provided shade and a cool drink on a hot summer day. Beth Puliti

grounds for purposes other than religion, but do not overlook churches as a resource when cycling abroad.

Markets

Outside of the United States it is more important to take into account the day of the week (and sometimes religion) when planning and gathering food. In many countries food stores and grocery markets are simply not open on Sundays. This of course varies by country, and even by city in some cases, but you will inevitably come across a shortage of food options in portions of Europe and Asia on a Sunday afternoon.

Markets abroad can offer a variety of culinary choices. Just be wary of sanitation procedures before purchasing. BETH PULITI

Fresh fruit and vegetables are abundant in many foreign countries and can be purchased for a fraction of the price compared to American grocery stores. BETH PULITI

Wildlife

The scenery is not the only thing that differs abroad. Often you will come across noticeably different wild animals as well. One of the most obvious differences is the abundance of wild cats and dogs in other countries. While a majority are harmless, it's worth keeping an eye out for them. Beyond this commonality the variation of wild animals and insects may differ noticeably between countries. Research your destination in advance to see if you'll need to be on the lookout for any potential pannier-raiding creatures.

In some places abroad, like the Balkans (above), you'll likely encounter ferocious and aggressive sheep dogs that will require rock throwing or other techniques to turn them away. This was the least threatening sheep dog we came across, so we were able to snap a photo. He still wanted to pursue the chase and attempt to bite, although he could likely only reach our ankles. BETH PULITI

Seeing wild monkeys (left) for the first time is exciting, but the allure wears off quickly when you see what a nuisance they can be, going after food from panniers and anywhere else they can find it. BETH PULITI

In Croatia you'll be hard-pressed to find a hotel sign, but pedaling the coastline you'll come across an abundance of "apartman" signs. Locate the landlord, take a look at the accommodations, negotiate a rate, and you'll be on your way to a good night's sleep.
BETH PULITI

Lodging

When on the hunt for where to lay your head for the evening, keep in mind that asking for a "campground" or "hotel" may not always lead to the answer you are looking for. In many countries lodging options fall outside the typical categories. In Croatia, particularly along the coast, you will find most lodging options labeled as "apartman." In Southeast Asian countries such as Malaysia and Thailand, you are most likely to find a "bungalow" or "resort" as your lodging options for the evening, so be careful how you phrase your inquiry when searching for shelter. Don't be intimidated by the sound of a "resort," though. More times than not in Southeast Asia, this can be a basic hotel room of varying character with a cost far below that of a basic hotel room in the United States—in some cases under $10 or $15.

Camping

Similarly, the simple act of camping is likely to be a bit different than you are accustomed to in the United States. Some countries, like Croatia, offer little to no camping infrastructure; other places, like certain regions of Italy, focus primarily on RV accommodations and entertainment; and still other countries,

Many foreign countries, like Albania, provide an abundance of beautiful wild camping options. BETH PULITI

like Albania and Norway, have an abundance of primitive camping spots where no one will bother you. The ability to wild camp outside of designated areas varies largely by country. If you are hesitant or uncertain if you will be breaking local laws, it is a good idea to do some Internet research about your destination in advance, and its stance on wild camping. One fail-safe way to ensure you are trouble-free is to ask the landowner or local authority before pitching your tent.

Water

Water quality abroad varies greatly, so while you might find the best-tasting water to grace your lips flowing from the tap in one country, you're likely to become immediately ill from drinking tap water in another country. There is no substitute for being prepared with treatment and remedies for when you sip from the wrong spout. Don't always do as the locals do. In the case of drinking water, it may be that they have developed an immunity from continued exposure to particular contaminates that would cause you to be immediately sidelined.

Pictures can be universal, so cards like these help communicate dietary restrictions and other important messages anywhere in the world. BETH PULITI

Picture Cards

With obvious language barriers, communicating with locals can often prove difficult. Even with English being the default second language for much of the world, as a touring cyclist seeking rural routes, communicating can be difficult outside of cities. Most of the communicating you will need to do concerns eating and sleeping, so one good backup plan to standardize your ability to communicate is to carry a few picture cards. As a vegetarian you might consider carrying small images of a cow, chicken, and pig crossed out and another card showing fresh vegetables. The combination of the two, along with a few hand gestures, typically affords a diet-safe meal in any country. For camping you can carry the same style card but with an image of someone sleeping in a tent—helpful for either finding a campground or seeking land-owner approval to wild camp on private land.

Standards? Not Everywhere . . .

While there are numerous details we recognize as standard in the United States, many do not necessarily transfer elsewhere. Two good examples within the world of bike touring are wheel size and camping stoves. While we may have the luxury of walking into a bike shop and finding bike tires and tubes in 26-inch, 27.5-inch, 29-inch, and a number of other sizes, this is not the case outside the United States. If you are looking for tube/tire availability in remote regions abroad, then 26 inches is your best bet. Camping stoves are another factor to consider when touring abroad. In many parts of the world, isobutene screw-on-style fuel canisters are not readily available, but various forms of gasoline, denatured alcohol, or methylated spirits can be found.

Charging Devices

No matter how simply you travel, it is likely that you will have at least one electronic device that will require charging—your phone for communication and taking photos—or you may be equipped with a number of devices like a GPS, phone, computer, and camera that will all require charging. In these cases be sure to check in advance what voltage your devices use and the voltage and type of outlets of your destination country. On other continents you'll need to bring (or purchase) a power converter to allow your chargers and devices to work with the local voltage and outlets.

Visas

For some foreign destinations a visa, in addition to a passport, may be required. The requirement for a visa varies depending upon your destination, citizenship, and duration of stay. A US citizen is able to travel internationally with the fewest restrictions of any nation. If a visa is required, the procedure and requirements can vary, with some needing advance paperwork and others obtainable on arrival (typically more common when arriving by air from the United States rather than arriving over land from a neighboring country). For more information about the requirements of your destination, visit travel .state.gov.

Vaccinations

Depending upon your destination it may be wise, or even required in some cases, to have certain vaccinations or medications prior to visiting other foreign countries. For rural parts of Southeast Asia, you'll want to be equipped with malaria medication. If you are touring in the Balkans, where sheep dogs and wild dogs are known to be particularly aggressive, it is wise to have rabies shots in advance. Local travel clinics in the United States can recommend which vaccinations you need, and can administer the shots or write prescriptions. In addition to a number of other helpful resources, travel.state.gov is a great place to reference for suggested and required immunizations prior to entering a specific foreign destination.

Signs of recent warfare are all-too-common in some foreign destinations. While unfamiliar to most, bunkers dot much of the Albanian countryside. BETH PULITI

Travel Insurance

To carry, or not to carry, travel insurance—that is always the question. Travel insurance can be a lifesaver when a trip goes horribly wrong. Depending upon the policy it can cover things like flight delays, missing luggage, canceled travel, hospitalization, evacuation, and more. The downside? For budget travelers, travel insurance can add a substantial expense to the cost of a foreign touring endeavor. Before committing to the additional expense, it is best to first evaluate how you might be covered through your current providers. The combined coverage of your personal health insurance, employer health insurance, homeowners/rental insurance, credit cards, and frequent traveler programs may provide enough coverage to get by and peace of mind that you and your possessions are protected abroad. If you do, however, decide to purchase travel insurance, there are a number of companies to consider, including Travelex and Cigna, or evacuation coverage plans through American Alpine Club memberships, GEOS, or even through DeLorme or SPOT service providers. Be sure to read the fine print of the proposed policy in detail. In some cases the activities you plan to partake in may be considered high risk and excluded from coverage.

CHAPTER SIX

Tips for the Long Haul

A bike tour for some can be a sub-24-hour excursion, a weekend away, or a weeklong vacation exploring a new destination. No matter the distance, bike touring and bikepacking provide an escape from the routine of your daily life and a chance to explore on your own terms. Some lucky people are able to pull off extended tours lasting weeks, months, or even years—across countries, continents, or even around the world. Long-distance touring, however, has additional factors and challenges to consider. Among those who have logged thousands of miles while living off the bike, you'll find a number of consistencies and tricks for an extended life on the road.

You may not need a cycling computer on shorter trips, but it can be a useful tool for navigating on longer trips. It also provides a sense of accomplishment as you click off the kilometers/miles. JUSTIN KLINE

Long-term Travel Mentality

By far the most important consideration for a long-distance touring trip is the mental aspect. Being away from home, friends, family, and all the typical comforts of home is a challenge for even the heartiest soul. The extent to which this mental challenge affects bike travelers varies, but the mentality required to endure life on the road remains the same. Not everyone will understand what you are doing and why you are doing it, and luckily they don't have to, because that is all up to you. People will say, "Wow that is cool. Aren't you tired of traveling yet? What is it like to be on vacation for so long? What is it like to be rich?" All very entertaining and sometimes engaging inquiries, but in the case of long-term bike travel, the reality is you are not on a vacation, but rather choosing to live an alternative lifestyle. Most people cannot even fathom such a lifestyle change, and even fewer are willing to make the sacrifices. Having the proper perspective and keeping it within reach are key to enduring the mental challenge of long-term travel. For more on the subject, and to encourage a long-term travel stint, *Vagabonding* by Rolf Potts is a great read.

Popular Touring Bits & Pieces of Gear

If you've bumped into a world bike traveler or two, chances are you see a pattern in the type of gear they are carrying. When you are traveling by bike on a daily basis, your gear can really take a beating over the course of years, or even just months. Those who live the nomadic cycling lifestyle know this well, and because of this there are a handful of items that have become staples for their long-term reliability on the road. Here are a few items that you'll likely find among the setup of a long-term touring cyclist:

Brooks leather saddles—After the first 2,500 miles (4,000 kilometers) of my most recent tour, I made the switch to a leather saddle and have not looked back since. A natural leather saddle takes the shape of your body over time, resulting in increased comfort over the long haul.

Ortlieb panniers—It's hard to find touring cyclists pedaling the globe and not using an Ortlieb bag these days, and for good reason. Their bags are known to be supremely waterproof and durable over the long haul. Their panniers and handlebar bags have proven reliable over the years, but there are less expensive options if you are on a budget.

Avid BB7 mechanical disc brakes—Once reserved for mountain bikes, you can finally find numerous touring-capable bikes with disc brakes these days. For performance and reliability the Avid BB7 mechanical disc brakes are hard to beat. The performance is similar to higher-priced hydraulic models, and the cable actuation ensures they are easy to adjust and service in remote areas.

Schwalbe Marathon tires—Those out for the long haul look for puncture resistance and long-wearing rubber, and that is where these tires are known to shine. It is not uncommon to hear of touring cyclists putting over 6,200 miles (10,000 kilometers) on Schwalbe Marathon tires with sufficient tread remaining.

While these items are by no means the only options on the market to consider, they are commonly used for long-distance bike travel—something to keep in mind if you are fortunate enough to embark on a long-distance cycling adventure.

Alternative Handlebars

When your hands are on the handlebars daily for an extended period of time, the ability to have and use multiple hand positions becomes especially important. For some the offerings of a stock drop-style handlebar or flat bar are simply not enough, and repetitive strain in the same position can cause long-term hand numbness or limited mobility. In addition to drop bars and straight flat bars, there are a number of alternatives, such as mustache bars, trekking (or butterfly-style) bars (popular in Europe), and alternative-style mountain bike bars. Here are some models worth considering:

Modolo Yuma—Multi-position trekking-style bar from Italy

Jones—Available as a loop or open style, offering a number of hand positions and mounting points. Suitable for on or off-road touring.

Nitto Mustache Bar—Mustache-style bar providing a more upright body position and multiple hand positions

Surly Open Bar—Alternative-style mountain bar

Salsa Woodchipper—Versatile drop-style bar suitable for off-road touring

Salsa Bend 2—Alternative-style mountain bar

On-One Mary—Alternative-style mountain bar

On-One Midge—Versatile drop-style bar suitable for off-road

If swapping to an alternative-style handlebar, keep in mind your stem length may need to be adjusted, and you'll need to ensure the clamp diameter of your stem and shifters remains compatible. On flat and alternative-style bars, you can also look to increase ergonomics with Ergon grips. You can also add foam grips or other layers of padding to help soften the strain of repetitive vibration and impact.

Compared to straight mountain bike bars, alternative-style bars like the Salsa Woodchipper can provide additional hand positions, which are helpful on longer journeys. Salsa Cycles

Bungee cords can make adding provisions easy, such as fresh roadside coconuts in Thailand. BETH PULITI

Bungee Cords or Voile Straps

The real estate on the back of your rack is valuable space. You can make it even more versatile by bringing along a few bungee cords or Voile straps for carrying provisions obtained along the way. A container of water, a six pack of beer, a bag of chips, even fresh fruit, all can find a temporary home on the back of your bike with the help of a bungee cord or Voile straps. In addition to carrying gear as your load fluctuates, they are also helpful for securing wet clothes to dry as you ride. Bungee cords are best used with caution though. If not secured properly, or if left hanging, they can quickly become entangled in your wheel, stopping you in your tracks.

Electronic Documents

When traveling for an extended period of time, things are bound to get lost. Hopefully those things are not important documents, but it can happen. It is wise to travel with images of important documents that could be lost or stolen such as your driver's license and passport, credit cards and the contact information on the back of the card, bank contact information, health insurance information, and important contact numbers. Redundancy is key, so use electronic storage such as flash drives, e-mail, Dropbox, and other cloud-based storage that allows access to these documents from anywhere. (As with all personal information, you should ensure that these images are stored in a secure location.) You can also download PDF manuals and other important documents rather than carrying paper versions to save weight. Make sure to leave copies of your passport and driver's license with someone at home, too.

Securing Your Bike

On shorter bike excursions the security of your bike is seldom an issue, but when you are traveling for an extended period of time, scenarios where you need to secure your bike are inevitable. For its balance of weight, security, and flexibility, a long cable lock is very practical, allowing you to easily secure your front wheel, frame, and rear wheel to a variety of fixed objects. Cable weight varies with thickness, so choose according to the security level that might be required for your intended destinations.

Tip: If touring frequently through urban areas, it is worth considering a set of locking skewers to secure your front wheel, rear wheel, and seatpost. A key is required to remove them, rather than a quick release or allen wrench.

Shopping (Dry) Bag

When touring for an extended period of time, through diverse destinations, your food load is bound to fluctuate. Rather than relying on plastic grocery bags, it is nice to bring your own dry bag or ultralight backpack, such as a small, collapsible silicon-impregnated (sil) nylon daypack, to not only gather food at markets, but also keep it dry when it is on top of your touring rack.

Chamois Cream

Continuous days and weeks in the saddle can lead to chafing and other issues for some cyclists. Consider products like chamois cream to lubricate below your belt and keep things comfortable on the saddle.

Supplements

Joint pain, particularly of the knees, can plague long-distance touring cyclists due to the increased weight and long-term repetitive motion. A supplement like glucosamine can go a long way toward eliminating or keeping knee and other joint pain at bay. Turmeric and arnica are other great supplements to carry, as they are natural ways to reduce inflammation and pain.

Don't Be Afraid to Take a Break

When traveling on a long-distance cycling trip, the desire to call it quits is natural. Days on end of soaking rain, broken components leaving you stranded, saddle sores, travelers' diarrhea, heat exhaustion, repeated flat tires, homesickness—any one of these challenges is enough to make even the toughest of road warriors question what they are doing. The key to not getting discouraged is simply to give it time. It might just be that some stationary time—a day, week, or even a month—to provide perspective is all you need to get back on the bike and explore further. Also keep in mind that the first week is often the toughest, as your body and mind break in and get used to the new routine.

Just one of the many rainy days you'll likely encounter over a long-distance tour. They may be frustrating at the time, but they're always worth it. BETH PULITI

CHAPTER SEVEN

Bike Maintenance on the Road

One of the most daunting elements of bike touring is the potential for something mechanical to go wrong, and the necessity of dealing with the maintenance while on the road. Fortunately, catastrophic issues seldom occur, and minimal bike maintenance skills are needed before departing on an overnight cycling adventure. Don't be afraid to set out knowing only a few basic maintenance items, such as inflating your tires, lubing your chain, and changing a flat. Odds are these are the only skills you'll need on a short cycling tour. For additional skills the Internet offers an abundance of resources that can be referenced beforehand, or even from the road if needed. Here are a few web-based resources that can help you become a sufficient mechanic while on the road, and in some cases provide downloadable guides for reference:

Sheldon Brown	sheldonbrown.com
Park Tools	parktool.com
Free bike repair book	freebikebook.blogspot.com

Repairing on the road requires being equipped with the proper tools and parts beforehand. Depending upon the length of your trip, the road/trail conditions, and the remoteness of your route, your tool and spare parts kit will vary. Here are some general guidelines for useful items to include in a basic kit, long-distance kit, and expedition kit.

Basic Kit

Multi-tool—equipped with 2mm–6mm allen key tools is a must. For longer journeys you'll likely want an 8mm and 10mm as well. Look for an included chain tool or carry a separate chain tool for easier use.

Fixing a flat tire will likely be your most common, and possibly only, repair while touring.
BETH PULITI

Emergency repair items like zip ties and hose clamps can save the day. The combination of the two allowed me to make it to the next town in rural Turkey to find a replacement bolt.
BETH PULITI

Separate allen key tools can be easier to use, but may add weight. Check to ensure the tool(s) you bring along are sufficient for most bolts on your bike. Keep in mind some jobs could require two individual tools at the same time.

Patch kit—Virtually weightless and indispensable

Tire boot—Also virtually weightless; a trip saver for sidewall tears and other sizable gouges in tires

Spare tube(s)—Two is typically sufficient

Pump—Look for a model that can be used as a mini floor pump for longer trips

Duct tape—Can serve as a temporary repair for a wide variety of gear

Zip ties—Helpful for securing gear; can replace anything from a broken bolt to a broken strap

Chain lube—Keeps your drivetrain running smooth and quiet

Long-Distance Kit

In addition to the basic kit, longer and more remote cycling adventures may require these additional items:

Hose clamps—Work nicely as a stronger repair solution. Carry sizes that accommodate your frame diameter and other gear, usually ¾ inch to 1¾ inches.

Replacement cleat and bolts—It is not uncommon to lose a cleat or bolt in your shoe, which makes it impossible to ride with clip pedals.

Parachute cord—Helpful for mending gear, as a clothesline, and for securing loose items

Replacement shifter and brake cable—Helpful to resolve shifting or brake issues or failure from potential corrosion, separating, or cut cables

Brake pads—On longer trips, particularly in wet and gritty conditions, brake pads can quickly deteriorate. Replacing pads on the road is simple and ensures you can descend safely.

Spare spokes—When preparing for a longer journey, determine the spoke lengths your wheels use. There could be as many as three different spoke lengths. Even if you don't know how to repair a wheel, it is helpful to have the spokes. In a pinch you can navigate the task with a downloaded tutorial or provide the spokes to a local mechanic or shop.

Tip: Store spare spokes in your seat tube with some strong tape and they'll stay straight and out of the way.

Sewing kit—For mending torn clothing, panniers, and other gear

Quick link—Can simplify resolving broken chains and help maintain ideal chain length

Chain pins—Tiny, but a trip saver for a devastated chain, particularly if a pin is lost when attempting to fix a broken chain

Loctite—Helpful for securing bolts prone to loosen over time from vibration, particularly rack bolts

Making roadside repairs can be awkward. Look for a low-hanging branch to lift the rear wheel off the ground and create a natural work stand. BETH PULITI

Seam grip—Useful for plugging water and airtight holes in your tent, rain gear, inflatable mattress, and other items

Spoke wrench—A basic one may already be included on your multi-tool, but a stand-alone spoke wrench can make the task easier without adding much weight

Expedition Kit

Looking to be able to do it all from the road? Here are some additional items that hopefully are rarely needed, but are much appreciated if catastrophe strikes and the need for a significant repair in a remote area arises:

Mini cassette tool—Allows you to not only replace your cassette, but also access drive-side spokes on your rear wheel if they need to be replaced

Cone wrench—Helpful if you need to tighten your hubs or access wheel bearings

Stove repair/cleaning kit—Over time, daily wear can lead to stove components deteriorating, particularly on stoves accommodating multiple fuel sources and especially if you are using gasoline as your stove fuel. Replacement O-rings can make a drastic improvement in your stove's function and efficiency.

Grease—Bearings, bolts, and fittings can eventually dry out. A little grease ensures things continue to run smooth and quietly.

Spare tire—Sometimes a tire is damaged beyond what a tire boot can mend, or on long journeys the added weight of gear may accelerate tire wear beyond expectations. These situations are when a spare tire is indispensable, especially in remote locations. Look for a folding-bead tire that is lightweight and compact to carry.

CHAPTER EIGHT

Off-the-Bike Gear

Bike touring and bikepacking combine cycling skills and gear with outdoor skills and gear, so even if you are an expert on the bike, there are a number of things to consider when assembling your touring setup. Your kit will likely vary depending on the type of bike touring trip; however, most of the camping gear will likely remain the same, as will the clothing. If you are road touring/credit card touring, then you may not need any of these overnight items and instead may want to carry a few additional items like flip-flops or town shoes and town clothes. As usual, functionality, weight, comfort, and packability should play into all these decisions.

In windy weather, stake out the upwind sides of the tent first. This will help spread the tent out so you won't have to fight the wind. Justin Lichter

Shelters

Shelters come in a variety of forms, from full-scale four-season tents to ultra-lightweight Cuben Fiber tarps. There are a range of features and designs and a gamut of options available. We'll briefly touch on the basics of the various concepts and give some pros and cons of each.

Tents

Tents come in all shapes and sizes and with all sorts of options and bells and whistles. Some people love tents and don't want to strip down to a tarp or tarptent. On a long-distance bike tour, it is very important to sleep well, since that is the time when your body recovers from all the activity you are doing. If you have trouble sleeping in the backcountry or need the extra luxury of a tent, then we highly recommend bringing a tent along. If you are adaptable and sleep well anyway and anywhere, then you are a good candidate for a lighter, more packable option, like a tarp or tarptent.

Pros:

Good for a variety of weather conditions including windy, super stormy weather

Fully bug proof

Generally pretty straightforward and easy to set up

Can choose a suboptimal camping spot and still be fairly well sheltered

Provides a bit more security and cover in an indiscreet campsite

Cons:

Heavier than other options and not as packable

Tent pole can be annoying and unwieldy to deal with and pack

Although not common, tent pole can break and create setup issues

Can get a lot of condensation on the inside of the tent depending on conditions

Tarptent

A **tarptent** is similar to a tent but is usually single walled or a hybrid style, meaning the rain protection layer is the main layer in places. There usually isn't an overlap of nylon and mesh throughout the whole body of the tent. This often shaves a lot of weight but can also lead to increased condensation depending on the climate and the conditions. Some tarptents can be set up without a tent pole, saving even more weight. They can also be strung up to a tree or your bicycle in order to provide the structural support.

A couple of different shapes of ultralight tarps made by Mountain Laurel Designs.
Justin Lichter

Pros:
Lighter and more packable than tents; some don't need tent pole
Full bug protection
Provides a bit more security and cover in an indiscreet campsite

Cons:
Can sag and be flimsy, especially in wet weather
Can have bad condensation in wet or humid weather like on the
   East Coast

Tarps
Tarps are the lightest and most packable shelter option. When we refer
to tarps, we don't mean the big blue tarps sold at Walmart and hardware
stores. These are special outdoor shelters that come in a variety of fabrics
and shapes and sizes. The typical and most affordable fabric is sil nylon.
These are fairly durable for their weight and are waterproof, although you
may want to seal the seam(s) before use. Lighter than sil nylon is Spinnaker
and Cuben Fiber. Spinnaker tends to lose its water repellency faster than
sil nylon and Cuben Fiber. Cuben Fiber is very lightweight and also very
durable for its weight, but much more expensive. Tarps come in a variety of
shapes ranging from ones that set up as A-frames to others that are pyramid
shaped. Which is better depends on personal preference.

Pros:
Super lightweight and packable, with no need for a tent pole
Can see out and watch the stars at night
Easy to set up once you get used to it
Typically no condensation issues if set up at the right height
Can safely and easily cook underneath it

Cons:
No bug protection unless you buy a separate system to go inside
Not fully enclosed so some people don't sleep well inside
May take time to get used to setting it up in less than ideal conditions
Need to be a bit more conscious of choosing a good campsite, especially one
    with good drainage

Tip: For bikepacking we usually prefer the A-frame-shaped tarp because it packs smallest and is easiest to set up between two trees or by using a bike propped against a tree. It also provides the most space for the weight. You can buy bug inserts made specifically to fit under this shaped tarp. On the other hand, pyramid-shaped tarps are better at dealing with wind and stormy weather, and are good choices if you are expecting nasty weather.

Tip: A tarp saves you the weight of a fabric floor since tarps don't have floors. We recommend bringing a lightweight polycro groundsheet or piece of Tyvek, which only weighs 1 to 3 ounces, to go under your sleeping pad and sleep system to protect your pad from moisture and dirt.

Sleeping Bags

There is nothing like getting into your sleeping bag after a tough day of riding. Climbing in your bag, stretching out, and elevating your feet is a fantastic feeling. Everybody sleeps differently and has different comfort levels, but following is what you need to know to choose a good bag.

Fill Materials

Down: This is the fluffy under-plumage from a goose or duck. Down is a great insulator. Most down in outdoor gear is goose down because it has a higher fill power. Fill power is the number of cubic inches that 1 ounce of down will displace. The higher the fill power, the less down is needed to meet a given temperature rating.

The manufacturer needs less down to make a higher-fill-power sleeping bag, but the price will still usually be higher. The higher the fill power, the less the bag will weigh. (Depending on their fill power, two different sleeping bag models with identical temperature ratings can have different weights.)

Asleep in down sleeping bags inside a tarp with bug-proof netting lining the inside. Justin Lichter

Pros:

Very light, highly compressible, durable, and breathable

Lasts a long time if you treat it right; the loft lasts longer than synthetic fill

Cons:

Initially more expensive

When wet, down loses loft and therefore its insulating properties. (Most quality down bags have a nylon fabric with a durable water repellence [DWR] coating to help keep water out; the shell of a few bags are even made of a completely waterproof, breathable membrane.)

Synthetic: There are many different brands of synthetic fill; however, they all fall under two main categories: short staple fills and continuous filament fills.

Short staple fills, like Primaloft, are the most common. They use densely packed strands of fine denier filaments to insulate. That means little fibers are packed together to create loft and insulation. Since the filaments are small, it allows for a flexible and fairly compressible synthetic bag. However, the fibers can break and lose performance quickly.

Continuous filament fills, like Climashield, are typically stronger and more durable. They are made from thicker, continuous fibers. Continuous filament fills have good loft, but because of that are less compressible.

Pros:
Cheaper
Fill is very evenly distributed
Completely non-allergenic
Maintains some insulating properties even when wet

Cons:
Lower warmth to weight ratio
Heavier than down and less compressible
Made out of polyester, which is petroleum-based and less sustainable
Usually doesn't last as long as down and doesn't fluff up as well

Tip for best loft/insulation: If you can, unpack your sleeping bag when you first stop for the night, instead of waiting until getting ready to sleep, so the bag has time to decompress, which adds more loft. If it's nice out during the day, air out your sleeping bag during a break. This will help keep it dry and lofty for when you need it later and it's too cold to dry out then.

Tip: If you are planning to purchase your first sleeping bag or only have one bag in your quiver, think about what time of year and where you will most likely be touring. For most people a 20-degree bag is a good trade-off and a good temperature rating that will work for most of the year. If you sleep warm and wear some clothes in the bag, you may be able to use a 30-degree bag as a three-season bag.

Temperature Ratings
Choose a sleeping bag rated for the coldest temperature you expect to encounter. There are a few ways to save weight and use a lighter-weight and warmer bag, which we'll mention later. The bad news is ratings are usually pretty subjective to each manufacturer. However, the new European Norm (EN) is helping to standardize the rating system—although not many manufacturers have adopted it yet—and it should become more common.

Traditionally a bag's temperature rating has been the lowest temperature at which the supposedly average sleeper is comfortable. This is tricky because everybody sleeps differently and has different metabolic rates. I am a warm sleeper and have used a summer sleeping bag liner down to 15 degrees F (not ideal, but it worked and I didn't freeze). Women usually sleep colder. Essentially manufacturers' ratings are based on their own research and categorization, so these numbers should be considered more of a guide than a guarantee.

Sleeping Bag Liners

Sleeping bag liners have a couple of uses. First, they help keep your sleeping bag cleaner so you can wash it less, which probably helps it last longer. Second, a liner often adds between 5 to 15 degrees of warmth to your sleeping system.

Some liners claim to add 25 degrees of warmth, but it depends on what they are made of. You can sleep in just a sleeping bag liner in hot weather, so it also gives your sleeping system more flexibility. Sometimes rectangular sleeping bag liners are called travel sheets.

Here are the popular types of sleep liners:

Silk: The lightest-weight and most compact. Insulates in cold weather and breathes and absorbs moisture in warm weather. Generally expensive.

Cotton: Durable and absorbs moisture well. Not very lightweight or compact and takes longer to dry. Reasonably priced.

Fleece and micro-fleece: Warmer and moisture wicking, although usually heavier and not very compact. Moderately priced.

Synthetics (Coolmax and MTS): Moisture wicking and breathable. Moderately priced.

Insulated (Thermolite Reactor Extreme): This liner can make your sleeping system 25 degrees warmer. Dries faster than cotton. Price ranges from moderate to expensive.

Tip: You can add a sleeping bag liner inside or a bivy bag over your sleeping bag to add 5 to 15 degrees to your sleeping system. This creates a versatile system that allows you to sleep comfortably in multiple temperatures with only one midweight sleeping bag. Some sleeping bag liners or bivy bags are very lightweight and packable. For example, a bivy made out of lightweight nylon and Cuben Fiber weighs only a couple of ounces and packs down smaller than a fist. Also, your shelter will dictate how exposed to the elements you are and play a large part in the warmth of your sleep system. A fully enclosed tent typically adds around 10 degrees to your sleep system since it keeps warmer air inside and also provides a barrier against any wind.

Tip: For all bikepacking and bike touring trips, we recommend a high-quality down sleeping bag. Down is much lighter and more packable. Pack your sleeping bag either in a waterproof stuff sack or waterproof pannier so its warmth is not vulnerable to water.

Tip: On a bike tour where you are going hotel to hotel, hut to hut, or hostel to hostel, you might not need a sleeping bag, but instead can carry just a sleeping bag liner. A liner can be nice in these situations and packs down really small.

Sleeping Bag Maintenance

Restoring DWR: The DWR on a sleeping bag will wear off over time. This is pretty easy to restore with a standard DWR treatment like Revivex Air Dry Waterproofing Spray.

Treating leaking down: All bags will lose a few feathers here and there. Most manufacturers use a tightly woven material for the shell or a down-proof liner to help prevent this. But it is inevitable that a bog will lose some feathers. Sometimes they're lost at the seams, other times the quills poke through the shell or liner. If this is happening, try to grab the feather through the opposite side of the sleeping bag and pull it back into the bag. The hole should be small and close up after the feather is pulled back inside; if not, the feather is destined to come out, but the loss of a few feathers won't affect the bag's performance. If you're losing feathers because of a rip in the shell material, or even something bigger than a small hole with a protruding feather, then you need to fix it as soon as possible.

Treating fabric tears: If you are out bikepacking or touring use a patch of nylon repair tape or some Tenacious tape. We carry a little bit of Tenacious tape and duct tape for scenarios like this. The Tenacious tape works really well for gear repairs since it sticks amazingly and comes off without leaving any residue, unlike duct tape.

Broken zipper: It's pretty easy to replace a slider; however, if the coil is damaged, then the repair becomes more complicated. Getting it professionally done by a gear repair service or tailor is recommended because the whole coil must be removed and replaced with a new one (which is pretty hard to do in the field).

To replace the zipper slider: Get a slider that matches the one you are removing. Letters printed on the slider tell you the size you need. If the stop and end is sewn into the bag, use a seam ripper to carefully remove stitching around the lower ends of the zipper tabs. When the zipper's end is visible, pry off the metal stop at the bottom of the zipper. Take care to not tear the tape at the base of the zipper teeth, as it can unravel.

With the stop off, slide the old zipper slider off. Take the new zipper slider and guide it onto the track tape (the coils or teeth). Start on the side the stop was on, if applicable. If there was a stop, replace it, then feed the opposite track tape in and test the zipper. If the stop was just sewn in, insert both track tapes into the top grooves of the slider, pushing them through to the slider's bottom. Use a pin if needed to work the track tapes through. Pull tapes gently to make sure the slider is sitting evenly on the tracks. With both tapes threaded through the slider, gently pull it up until the locked track teeth appear at the bottom; make sure they're even and track evenly.

If the metal zipper ends were sewn into the bag itself, sew a new stop at the top of the tracks with a needle and thread. Sew the zipper back into the sleeping bag, following the visible needle holes left from where the stitching was removed for repair.

Tips for a Little Extra Warmth on a Cold Night

- Find a campsite out of the wind and away from water.
- Pee before going to sleep. This helps keep your body warm.
- Boil some water, put it in a water bottle, and place the water bottle between your legs in the sleeping bag (make sure the bottle won't leak).
- Cinch up the hood on your sleeping bag. If it's really chilly, cinch it up until only your nose and mouth are exposed.
- Eat a snack.
- Wear extra layers to sleep—socks, too.
- Sleep on your side.
- Pull your beanie down as far as it will go on your head or over your face.

Sleeping Pads

Sleeping pads are not an absolute necessity, but they help with comfort, cushioning, and insulation. A sleeping pad keeps you from losing a lot of body heat to the ground. Without one you can get chilled no matter how warm your sleeping bag because the sleeping bag's loft is getting compressed underneath you, reducing its ability to insulate.

R-value: This is the measure of a pad's insulative properties. The higher the R-value, the more insulating it is.

Shape: Pads have different shapes. Some are contoured to your body's shape or tapered to help cut down on extra material, pack space, and weight. The type of sleeper you are (back, side, frequent roller, etc.) determines what shape pad you will want.

Sleeping Pad Types

The types of pads available range from foamies to inflatable pads. The choice is personal preference depending on how you typically sleep. If you can sleep anywhere and have no trouble sleeping on a hard floor, then you could get away with a thin foamie. If you are like the princess and the pea, however, you may need a thicker, full-length inflatable pad.

Self-inflating pads: These are pretty popular because of their comfort. They're usually made from open cell foam that's sealed inside an airtight, waterproof nylon shell.

Pros:
Comfortable with adjustable firmness
Insulative (good R-value)
Compact and very packable when not inflated

Cons:
Typically heavier than thin foam pads of the same size
Definitely more expensive
Can be punctured in the field, but it usually isn't too difficult to fix them

Air pads: Air pads use air for comfort and have to be blown up. Sometimes they have some foam or insulation incorporated into the pad for extra warmth.

Pros:
Comfortable
Compact when packed

Cons:
Can pop, but repairs usually are not too difficult
Require a lot of air to blow them up
Not as warm as other pads if uninsulated

Foam pads: These are basic pads made of closed-cell foam.

Pros:
Weight varies depending on size and thickness; can be very lightweight
Inexpensive
Durable
Good insulation

Cons:
Not as comfortable
Not as packable

Tip: Some companies make inflatable pillows. This is a completely unnecessary purchase that just adds extra weight and takes up space. Use your sleeping bag stuff sack or your frame or handlebar bag as a pillow at night by filling it with extra clothes. If you use a hydration bladder, you can add extra air to that and place it under your sleeping bag as another pillow option.

Tip: To find a hole or leak in an inflatable pad, submerge the inflated pad in soapy water. Remove the pad and with the valve closed try to push out the air. The soapsuds should bubble in the area with the leak and show you where you need to place the patch.

This is a typical ultralight cowboy camping setup, or sleep system, underneath a tarp. Note the polypro groundsheet, the tarp being used for a pillow, and the pack or hydration pack functioning as the lower half of the sleeping pad.
JUSTIN LICHTER

Cooking Equipment

Stoves

Backpacking stoves are standard equipment for bikepacking, but may be unnecessary for bike touring if you will be passing through towns often.

Some ultralighters don't cook meals or boil water, so they don't even bother carrying a stove. Some people are perfectly happy eating cold meals at night. That saves some extra space in your bags. I like to cook one meal a day (dinner). It gives me some variety in my food and something to look forward to at night.

If you are cooking on your biking trip, then get a stove for backpacking and not a car-camping stove. They are different. Backpacking stoves are lighter, smaller, and packable, and most only have one burner. If you carry a stove, it's ideal if the stove and all its necessary components fit inside your cooking pot.

There are three main types of stoves: canister stoves, liquid-fuel stoves, and alcohol stoves. There are also some alternative-fuel stoves too. Each stove type has pros and cons. Most people "watching their weight" use an alcohol stove for at least three seasons, if not year-round. I have used alcohol stoves in conditions as cold as –30 degrees F and at 18,000 feet elevation and haven't had any problems.

Learn how to clean and maintain your stove properly. This is mostly a concern with liquid-fuel stoves. Bring along a field maintenance kit if you're going out on an extended journey.

Cooking tip: Soaking certain foods before you cook them helps them cook faster and conserves fuel—or in some circumstances uses no fuel at all. For example, some people soak dried beans ahead of time and get away without carrying a stove and cooking equipment.

Alcohol Stoves

These are nice, simple, lightweight, quiet, and compact. There is nothing to go wrong, break, or clean. All you have to do is pour alcohol in the stove and light it. It burns slowly and will boil your water. You can make your own alcohol stove out of soda cans, tuna cans, or cat food cans. You can't beat that price!

Alcohol stoves don't burn as hot as other types of stoves, so it can take longer to boil water, especially if it's windy. With alcohol stoves you definitely want a windscreen. Depending on the type of alcohol stove you use, you may need a pot support or stand. You can use a few of your tent stakes for this.

Alcohol stove pros:

Easy to use, simple

Compact, lightweight

Fuel is easy to find and cheap

Stove itself is cheaper than any other stove, even if you buy the most expensive titanium alcohol stove

No parts to clean or break

Burns clean if you use the right fuel and leaves less soot on your pot

You can reuse any plastic bottle for a fuel bottle and refill it as often as you want

Alcohol stove cons:

Doesn't burn as hot as other stoves

Less fuel efficiency and flame control, especially in windy conditions

If you pour too much alcohol in the stove, it can be dangerous to blow out the flame. It's also difficult to pour leftover fuel back into your fuel bottle for later use. The Trangia alcohol stove is heavier but makes up for it with additional utility. You can snuff it out with the top and put a lid on to contain the unused fuel.

Sometimes in areas with summer fire bans, alcohol stoves are included in those bans.

Using a Trail Designs Calera Cone alcohol stove inside the tarp at night. Justin Lichter

Tips on using alcohol stoves in the cold: If you're camping in the cold with an alcohol stove and it won't light, hold the lighter to the alcohol for a longer period. Alternatively, light a piece of toilet paper and hold it above or drop it into the alcohol stove to act as a wick.

Tips on finding alcohol: Finding denatured alcohol in the United States is not difficult. Look for Heet, the gas-line antifreeze in the yellow bottle; it's methyl alcohol and burns cleanly, and is cheaper than denatured alcohol. Heet also comes in a red bottle, but it's isopropyl alcohol, which doesn't burn as cleanly as the methyl alcohol in the yellow bottle; it will blacken your pot too. If you're desperate, you can use rubbing alcohol, but it blows out easily and blackens your pot.

Finding denatured alcohol internationally is not as hard as a lot of people think. I have found it in every country that I've traveled in. The trick is to keep your eyes open and remember that you really just want methyl alcohol. In many countries methyl alcohol is used as a window cleaning fluid. It is dyed Barney purple so people won't drink it.

Alternative-Fuel Stoves

There are some stove options that don't really fit neatly into other categories. Most of these alternative-fuel stoves are ultralight options but aren't as popular as an alcohol stove.

Esbit tablet stoves: Fuel for these stoves are little white squares about the size of a shredded wheat biscuit. They light instantly when touched with flame and burn slowly. The stove consists of a little plate for the fuel tablet and a little titanium stand for your pot. The system is incredibly light. The main problem with the Esbit stove is that it is hard to find, as are the fuel tablets. It works well if you're doing mail drops, but places that sell Esbit stoves and tablets are few and far between.

Wood-burning stove: This stove is similar to an alcohol stove, but has a little fan that helps feed oxygen to the fire. You fuel the fire with little twigs, leaves, and other things you find that burn. The theory is you still have a stove, but don't have to carry fuel with you.

It's an interesting concept but won't work in all environments. On the East Coast there's enough wood, but it rains a lot. You may not always be able to find dry tinder, and you may not want to search for twigs at the end of a tiring day. Typically people using this system gather dry tinder as they come across it and carry it with them to start their fire at night. This of course can be a hassle. In addition, natural fires don't burn clean, making pots sooty and black, which can get your hands and other gear inside your pack dirty.

Canister Stoves

Canister stoves are fueled with a pressurized canister of isobutane or a butane/propane mix. You attach the stove to the canister by screwing it on, then open the stove valve and light it with a lighter or match and you're ready to go. Some canister stoves even have a starter button. They sound like a jet engine and boil water really fast. The fuel canisters are self-sealing, so when you detach them from the stove, the gas doesn't leak out.

Canister stoves burn clean and are easy to use. They also usually have decent flame control, allowing you to simmer or boil water for different needs. Also, you never have to prime canister stoves as with liquid fuel stoves.

While canister stoves heat your food quickly and are convenient in many ways, they have some issues other stoves don't. For instance, you may need a little more than one canister worth of fuel for your trip, but you can't fill a canister partway. So unless you have one from an old trip, you have to carry two full canisters, and they don't get smaller when they are empty. Also, since you can't refill a canister, it creates extra waste that ends up in a landfill. Canisters are more expensive than other fuels too. But most importantly, I have seen canisters depressurize in the cold—usually in below freezing temperatures. Depressurized canisters can lead to a weak burn until the canister warms up.

Using a canister stove outside the tarp in Nepal. Justin Lichter

Canister stove pros:

Easy to use

Fairly compact and lightweight, but not quite as light or compact as an alcohol stove

Good flame control

No spilled fuel or direct fuel handling

Burns clean; leaves little soot on pots

Maximum heat output right away

No priming

Canister stove cons:

Fuel is more expensive

Poor cold-weather performance

Heat output reduces over time; as the fuel is used in the canister, the pressure decreases

Difficult to tell how much fuel and how many uses are left in a canister

Harder to find canisters for resupply

Cold weather tip for canisters: In cold weather you can keep the canister warm by putting it in your sleeping bag at night (which works well if you boil water in the morning). Shortly before stopping for the evening, place it in a jacket pocket to warm the fuel up. You can also put your canister in water in your pot lid. The water (as long as there is no ice) is above freezing and will warm the canister just enough to get it out of that inefficient temperature range. Don't put it in hot water to warm it up it. The gas might expand too much.

Some models are unstable because their base is small and they're tall stoves with a high center of gravity, making them more tip-prone, especially since you add weight at the top when cooking. This can definitely make it unstable, but you can counter this with a plastic stabilizer that widens the base area and reduces the chance of knocking over your stove and spilling your dinner.

I.S.S. (Integrated Stove Systems): Some popular canister stove systems, like the Jetboil systems and MSR Reactor, sell the stove and cooking pot or cup as an integrated system, and often add a few other things to the kit. The Jetboil Flash includes a stabilizer system, a coffee press, and some other gadgets.

I.S.S. stove systems compared to traditional canister systems:

I.S.S. stove pros:

Offer some of the fastest boil times

High fuel efficiency

All-in-one package means you don't have to purchase additional cookware

I.S.S. stove cons:
Less versatility (especially when traveling as a group)
More expensive
Not as lightweight as ultralight options like alcohol stoves

Canister stove considerations: *Never* use a windscreen on a canister stove where the stove attaches directly to the canister. This can cause over-heating and prohibits airflow, which can cause the fuel to explode. You can use a windscreen with canister stoves that allow you to have the canister unattached to the stove itself. A remote canister can also be turned upside down to add pressure to the fuel as the canister as it becomes empty.

Some models have internal pressure regulators to keep gas pressure consistent as the canister empties. It also helps cold weather performance.

Some canister stoves have stabilizers, with others you have to buy them separately. Stabilizers are usually a piece of plastic that attaches to the fuel canister's bottom creating a wider base to prevent the whole stove from tipping over.

Tip on canisters: Most canisters use a Lindal valve and standardized threading so you can use them between brands, even though the stove manufacturer recommends that you only use their brand of canister. For example, you'll have no problem using an MSR or Gigapower canister on a Jetboil stove.

Liquid-Fuel and Multi-Fuel Stoves

Liquid-fuel stoves are also common with outdoor groups and backpackers, but not as popular with lightweight hikers/bikepackers due to their weight. In the United States these stoves use a refillable fuel bottle that's filled with white gas.

These stoves perform really well in extremely cold temperatures, but they need to be manually pumped to pressurize them and primed to vaporize the fuel. Most liquid-fuel stoves can use a variety of fuel sources like white gas, kerosene, unleaded gasoline, diesel, and even jet fuel. Check the manual to make sure the stove actually is a multi-fuel stove and which fuels it can burn.

Fuel Choices

White gas is the cleanest fuel. If you burn other fuels besides, you will need to clean the stove more often.

White gas pros:
Cleanest and most efficient liquid fuel choice
Evaporates quickly when spilled

Using a multi-fuel stove in a small Nepali village. In some international settings the option to use various fuels can be very handy. JUSTIN LICHTER

White gas cons:
Spilled fuel is very flammable
Priming is required

Unleaded gasoline and diesel pros:
Common anywhere

Unleaded gasoline and diesel cons:
Spilled fuel is flammable and smells
Need to prime the stove and clean it more often

Kerosene pros:
Spilled fuel is less likely to ignite
Commonly available fuel source

Kerosene cons:
Spilled fuel evaporates slowly and smells
Need to prime the stove

Liquid-fuel stove pros:
Best option for cold-weather performance
Refillable fuel bottle
Works with multiple fuels

Fuels are fairly cheap and can be found almost anywhere

Stable stovetops can handle large cookware

Liquid-fuel stove cons:

Requires priming, which increases the likelihood of fuel spills

Expensive

Heavier than ultralight options

Components, including the fuel bottle, are usually sold separately.

Tips on multi-fuel jets: If you are using a multi-fuel stove, it's likely to have jets designed specifically for the different types of fuel it can burn. Make sure you use the right jet piece for the fuel source you plan to use. Also, on your fuel bottle in a permanent marker, write out which jet goes with what type of fuel in case you lose the instruction manual.

Tip on using unleaded gasoline: If you plan to run your multi-fuel stove on unleaded gasoline, use the lowest octane fuel available. It burns more efficiently and cleaner than higher-octane fuels and will save you some money. However, you'll still have to clean it more often than running it on white gas.

Maintenance tip: If you plan on using a liquid-fuel stove, learn how to clean and maintain it, and review the instructions before a trip. Learning how to maintain the stove while it's clean is much easier than learning on the trail when your stove won't work and you're hungry after a long day of riding.

Priming tip: We've seen many people almost burn down shelters and cabins while trying to prime their liquid-fuel stoves. But priming a liquid-fuel stove is not difficult and doesn't have to create an eyebrow-singing fireball—just read the instructions and practice in a safe environment, like on a cement patio or sidewalk.

Priming a stove entails letting a little bit of liquid fuel into a dish on the stove and lighting it to preheat it. That way when you turn the stove on full blast, the gas vaporizes. Also make sure you know how to turn the gas off quickly in case things get out of hand.

Other Considerations for Stoves

- Never cook inside your tent. You can burn down your tent while you are inside it and risk getting carbon monoxide poisoning.

- Make sure all fuel lines, valves, and any other connections are tight before turning on the fuel and lighting your stove.

- Cook on flat or semi-flat areas.

- Keeping the lid on your pot while cooking will heat your food or boil water a lot faster. It also uses less fuel and water, so you won't need to carry as much water throughout the day (if you're not near a water source when camping).

- When possible, choose a pot that's wider than taller. It allows more contact area for the flame, increasing efficiency, and helps lower the cook system's center of gravity.

- New fuel canisters may have a small air pocket at the top, which must flow out for a second or two before the stove will light. It's important to avoid tipping over a canister stove, particularly when the canister is new, as it could cause a big flame-up.

- Don't fill the fuel bottle for a liquid-fuel stove above the bottle's fill line. If it's too full, you can't pressurize the fuel properly. Also, remember that fuel expands as it warms up, so if the bottle gets hot from being near the stove or on a warm day, filling it below the fill line will prevent too much pressure from building up.

- If you're trying to pump a bottle for a liquid-fuel stove but the pressure isn't building, remove the bottle's top and flay or spread out the rubber gasket that seals it to the bottle. The constant pumping can cause the gasket to pull away from the sidewalls thereby preventing friction and pressurization.

- If you're not planning to use your liquid-fuel stove for a while (several months or longer), empty the fuel bottle. Fuel can go bad over time.

- Consider using a heat exchanger with liquid-fuel stoves if you are headed out in the winter. It helps boil water and melt snow faster, and saves fuel.

Cookware

There are many different sizes and types of cookware. Some pots have lids that are a little heavier but can also be used as a sauté pan. The important things to keep in mind as you figure out what size and which system will work best for your trip are:

- How many people are in the group you're cooking with (or for)?

- If you're with a group of people, figure out if everybody's cooking separately or as a group. If cooking for yourself, you can save weight and space in your kit by eating out of your pot rather than a separate bowl or cup.

- Are you a backcountry gourmet or a "just eating to keep going" type person?

- Do you need a cookware set, or can you piece a good cookware system together with a pot and a spork?

- How much weight do you want to carry?

- Depending on how long you are biking, how much will you need to eat? (The longer your ride, the larger your protions will be.)

For cooking, each person should carry:

A pot to cook with and eat out of. A 0.9-liter pot usually works well for a single person. If you're in a group cooking communally, each person needs a bowl or cup. You also need to determine how many people in the group need to carry stoves and pots.

If carrying a pot, make sure it has handles. Some require a separate external handle, so make sure you have those.

Typical comparisons for people/cookware if you are cooking communally or alternating cooking.

Factor that 1 person will eat about 0.6 liter the first day or two and then up to 0.8 to 0.9 liter thereafter, to figure necessary total pot volumes		
1 to 3 people	1 stove	1 or 2 pots, depending on meals
3 to 5 people	1 to 2 stoves (if alcohol definitely 2 stoves), depending on what you are cooking	2 to 3 pots
5 or more people	2+ stoves (3+ if alcohol)	3+ pots

A spork or spoon: Use your pocketknife if you need to cut anything; don't bother carrying an extra knife for eating.

Cookware Materials

Titanium: Also known as Ti

Pros:
Lightweight, tough, and durable—one Ti pot could last your whole life
Top choice for weight watchers

Cons:
More expensive
Conducts heat less than other materials

Using a titanium pot as a cup, bowl, and cooking device narrows down the utensils needed on a trip.
JUSTIN LICHTER

Aluminum

Pros:
Lightweight, cheaper than Ti

Cons:
Dents and scratches easily
Breaks down slowly when used with acidic foods
Some people think cooking in aluminum is unhealthy. Cooking leafy greens and cauliflower in aluminum can change their taste and color. (That's kind of scary.)

Stainless Steel

Pros:
Tough, durable, and more scratch-resistant than aluminum

Cons:
Heavy
Can heat unevenly, causing burnt spots in the bottom of the pot

Plastic

Pros:
Lightweight, pretty durable and scratch resistant
Cheap

Cons:
Not as durable as metal products, can melt
Some plastics are stained by foods like tomato sauce

Other considerations: If you need coffee in the morning to get moving, it's a lot faster to boil water using a canister stove rather than an alcohol stove. If you plan to boil multiple times per day, this should be taken into consideration when choosing what equipment to bring.

Water

You never know the quality of water you'll find in the backcountry, so it's advisable to carry some sort of water treatment. Water treatment is a debatable topic because of the varying effect of waterborne illnesses on different people. Some people can forgo treating water and don't get sick and others get very sick right away. A full third of people are Giardia carriers and don't know it. It is more likely that after a certain level of contamination people get sick. Fortunately, contracting Giardia is rare, and in most cases people who believe they have Giardia simply have a small bacteria or stomach bug.

That said, you're still better safe than sorry. You never know which sources are contaminated, and getting a waterborne illness—or any illness for that matter—isn't fun, so use a water treatment system. Most weigh 8 ounces—less than a can of soda—or less, so they don't add much weight to your kit.

Tip: While contaminated water is often blamed, most backcountry illnesses probably aren't caused by drinking water. For instance, in well-traveled areas, people probably get sick from poor hygiene, improper hand washing, or cross-contamination. Most of that can be easily prevented. For instance, don't let people dig into your bag of trail mix; instead pour some into their hands. Simple things like that can keep you healthy. And when most people say they had Giardia, it was more likely a stomach bug caused by something in the water, but not technically Giardia.

The main culprits of waterborne illness, all of which can be taken care of with the proper treatment options, are:

Protozoan cysts (Cryptosporidium parvum, Giardia lamblia). Small (1 to 300 microns; one micron = one-millionth of a meter).

Bacteria (*Escherichia coli, or E. coli, Salmonella, Campylobacter jejuni, Yersinia entercolitica, Leptospira interrogans*, and many others). Really small (0.1 to 10 microns).

Viruses (hepatitis A, rotavirus, enterovirus, norovirus, Norwalk virus). Super small (0.005 to 0.1 micron). Only purifiers, not filters, eliminate viruses because they are so small. Viruses aren't typically found in North American backcountry water sources.

Some chemicals and other natural—and unnatural—things can make water taste bad, such as tannin from trees, cow pies, iodine, etc. No matter

You never know how good or bad a water source is going to be. This dead bat was in a much-needed source. JUSTIN LICHTER

your choice of water treatment, bringing along a few packets of electrolyte mix or other single-serving instant drink mix can make the taste more palatable.

With any water treatment you use, make sure that all parts of your water treatment system dry completely between trips—especially if you are using a filter. Take things apart and air them out; otherwise you could end up with mold on the filter, inside your water bottles, or somewhere else you're not likely to notice.

If you're using a filter, another way to eliminate some of the bad taste is with a carbon component. Some filters come with it and others offer it as an add-on. The carbon component gets rid of the taste when used at the appropriate time. If you're using a purifying filter system, don't use the carbon component too early, as it can deactivate the chemical treatment before it has fully treated the water.

Water Treatment Options

In North America you'll usually only need to filter water, which removes most threats in water, except for viruses. Purification, which includes pump- and gravity-based filters, boiling, ultraviolet light, mixed-oxidant solution pens, and chemical treatment, eliminates all biological hazards.

Evaluating Water Treatment Options

Treatment Evaluation	Speed	Weight	Size	Pore size	Convenience	Ease of use	Maintenance	Longevity	Durability	Quality of taste	Cost
Filters/Purifiers*	2	2	2-3	4	2	2-3	3*	3	3	5 (F), 3 (P)	$60-$220
Gravity filters	3	2	2-3	4	3	4	3	3	4	5	$65-$80
Squeeze bottles	3-4, can't chug, thin stream	3	3	3	4	4	2	3	3	5 (F), 3 (P)	$35-$50
UV light	5	4	4	NA	4	5	5	4	4	5	$79-$149
Mixed oxidant	4	3	4	NA	2-3	2-3	3	4	3	2-3	$140
Chemicals	1	5	5	NA	5	5	5	5	5	2-3	$6.50+

5 = Excellent, 4 = Very good, 3 = Good, 2 = Fair, 1 = Poor, NA = Not applicable   * Some filters are not cleanable.

Purifiers have to meet EPA standards for getting rid of viruses, bacteria, and protozoa; filters do not. For international travel you might want a purifier or an alternative water treatment method for this reason. In some cases you'll find filter-based purifiers filter water and then they add a chlorine solution to kill viruses.

Other treatment options include pump- and gravity-based filters and bottles with built-in filters. But remember, not all filters are purifiers and some purification options like pumps cost more than filters without purification.

Key factors for evaluating water treatment methods are effectiveness, speed, weight, size, pore size (only relevant for filters), convenience and ease of use, maintenance, lifespan and durability, impact on taste, and cost.

Filters

There are two main types of filters: pump filters and gravity filters. Pump filters are commonly used on the trail. Gravity filters are good for base camps, large groups, or if you're staying at a campground without running water. With the latter you just fill the bladder with water, hang it from a tree at night, and have fresh, filtered water to drink in the morning.

Always be proactive when using a water filter. When the flow becomes slow, clean it. Don't wait, as it will just take longer and longer to fill your water bottles, and it gets more frustrating. Plus keeping the filter clean helps it last longer.

Keep in mind that the insides of a filter can be fragile, so handle it with care when you are cleaning or using it, and be extra careful in freezing temperatures. When it is going to freeze at night, it's important to get rid of all the water from the filter and the filtering medium. If water is left inside it could freeze, expanding and cracking the filter cartridge.

Many water filters are designed for field maintenance. This helps because you can clean the filter rather than replacing it, but if you want to get the most out of your filter, consider cleaning it as soon as it gets harder to pump or the stream of pumped water lessens. If you're filtering silty water, you'll have to do this more often, which can be a pain.

To help reduce the amount of silt that hits the filter itself, many filters come with a pre-filter. Pre-filters can slow water intake, but if you're filtering silty water it's worth the effort to use a pre-filter or cover the intake tube's open end. If your filter doesn't come with a pre-filter, you can simply use a coffee filter or bandanna and secure it around the end of the intake hose with a rubber band.

Tip: Even if you don't use a filter, placing a bandanna, the bottom of your shirt, or a coffee filter over the mouth of your water bottle when you fill it can prevent silt and floating things from getting in your drinking water.

Chemical Treatment

Chemical treatments, like Aqua Mira or iodine, are a nice choice because they're lightweight and small; however, it takes time to fully treat water and they typically leave a residual taste.

Using chemicals to treat cold water takes longer than using them to treat warm water, and it takes longer to treat viruses and cysts with chemicals because they have "thick shells."

Tip: If you're at a nasty-looking water source, you might want to treat it twice or let the chemicals sit longer than normal.

Some ultralighters use household bleach for water treatment for its ease of access. It is basically chlorine, so it is similar to Aqua Mira, which uses chlorine dioxide, but is not FDA-approved. Chlorine, used improperly, is deadly, so this is not an advisable treatment technique for regular use, but could be used in a pinch.

SteriPEN

For the quickest and most effective water treatment option, check out ultraviolet light systems, like the SteriPEN. All you have to do is dip your water bottle in water, dip the device into the water, and swirl the water around for a minute or so. You can treat water while walking if you need to—there's no sitting around pumping water while mosquitoes snack on you.

Since the SteriPEN treats water so quickly, you can often carry less water since you can drink within a minute of getting to a water source, unlike a filter or chemical treatments, which can take notably longer to produce potable water.

You should know that although the SteriPEN sterilizes all the contaminants in your water, the rim of your water bottle could feasibly be contaminated, so be sure to use the

The SteriPEN uses a UV light that treats the water so it is safe to drink. Justin Lichter

squirt portion of your bottle to drink and do not allow unfiltered water to travel through the valve.

Read the instructions before you start using the SteriPEN—or any other water treatment system for that matter. There are typically indicators, such as waiting for the green light to flash before you stick it in the water, that make all the difference in the function of the product. If you know how to use your SteriPEN and are having problems with it, dry off its sensors a little or let it dry by leaving it out in the sun. Sometimes it can help to stick it in your pocket for a while before or after use.

Tip: When using a SteriPEN or other water treatment that uses a battery, and the user manual doesn't specify battery type, use lithium batteries. They are more expensive but last longer and work better in the cold. If you're having trouble with batteries in cold temperatures, treat your water at night before you go to sleep, since the batteries are still warm from the day, and you'll have clean water in the morning. Another option is to put the batteries or the entire water treatment device in your pocket for a little while to help warm it up before you need to use it.

Tip: If you are really worried about water quality and want to take full precautions, you need to go the full nine yards. It is possible while treating water to inadvertently do things that create potential cross-contamination from untreated water. It's best to assume all untreated water from streams, lakes, etc., has something harmful in it. If you use a filter, never allow the intake hose (the hose that goes into the water source) to touch the outflow (filtered water) hose, the inside of the filter, or your water bottle. Isolate the hoses in separate, marked ziplock bags, so no untreated water from the intake hose touches any other part of the filter.

If you use a SteriPEN, technically you cannot clean the threads (screw-top) of your water bottle, and you don't want to put your mouth to the water bottle to drink. Simply using a straw to drink and leaving it inside your water bottle can remove this possibility. Take the straw out when you fill your bottle and then drop it right back into the treated water after.

If you use chemicals to treat water, after 30 minutes or so, loosen the lid on your water bottle and turn it upside down. Make sure the treated water wets the threads and wait another 10 minutes or so before drinking. This disinfects the spout where you drink.

You may feel like a germaphobe, but this is how you take full preventative measures and treat your water to the full extent. After all, what's the point of taking all that time to pump water if you drink a few drops of highly contaminated water and get sick?

Preventative medication tip: If you're traveling where obtaining safe drinking water is an issue, you can bring along medication to treat potential illnesses. A doctor can prescribe medications like Metronidazole or Nitazoxanide to treat amoebic dysentery and Giardia as a precaution.

Tip on avoiding chemical contamination from water: No water treatment option removes chemical contamination effectively. It's best to avoid getting water from water sources near heavy agricultural runoff or current or abandoned mines.

Soap

Please don't use normal, or even backcountry biodegradable, soap in or near backcountry water sources. Most soap adds nutrients to water that can create algae blooms, encourage pathogen growth, or contaminate water. Instead carry some water away from the water source and rinse off there.

Headlamp/Bike Light

A good headlamp/bike light is a necessity for most cycling adventures. You never know when you are going to end up riding into the twilight trying to reach a town or looking for that elusive camping spot. In most cases, though, you'll find yourself riding during the day and relaxing in the evening, so a

Using a headlamp in camp at night to cook and look over the maps for the following day.
Justin Lichter

Headlamp, Light Features

Characteristic	Unit of measurement	Meaning
Light output/ brightness	Lumens	How bright the light is at its source. The higher the number, the brighter the light.
Beam distance	Meters	How far the unit's beam will illuminate a surface.
Run time/ battery life	Hours	At its lowest setting, how long the unit should be able to produce usable light.
Weight	Ounces or grams	Most headlamps are between 3 and 6 ounces. Heavy-duty, high-intensity lights are heavier.
Size	Inches or centimeters	The dimensions of the headlamp itself. Head-lamp straps are adjustable and should fit just about any head.

headlamp is typically sufficient for both camping and those rare on-the-bike illumination needs.

Lights should tell you their lumens (brightness), run time, weight, and beam distance. Compare the figures on a number of models to find out which offers the best combination of output, features, durability, and price.

Some models have multiple beam patterns creating both a flood and wide beam. Optics that produce a long-distance beam are ideal for moving at a higher rate of speed, such as while riding. A lower-illumination flood beam is ideal for reading, cooking, and other campsite activities.

For camping look for a colored LED—red is most commonly used—to preserve your night vision. A red LED is easier on your eyes because it doesn't make your pupils constrict, as a white LED does. They're also not as bright, so your light won't disturb your partner if you're up later at night.

Headlamp Modes
Most headlamps have a few different modes, or brightness levels. This helps conserve the battery when you don't need it on full force. Some also have a strobe feature that ensures you are noticed when riding later in the evening.

Regulated Output
Many new LED lamps feature regulated output. Instead of losing light as the batteries drain, they sustain their brightness throughout the life of the batteries. This is a great feature, but when the batteries reach a low point, the power fades quickly. A regulated headlamp also allows you to use lithium batteries, which offer prolonged output at the initial lumens, especially in cold weather.

CHAPTER NINE

Clothing

Your clothes are one of the most important components to your touring kit since you are always on the move without the protection of a permanent shelter. This requires a clothing kit that will keep you dry in the rain, warm in cold weather, and cool in hot weather. The key to a perfect clothing kit while bikepacking or touring is comfort and versatility. If a clothing garment can be used in only a specific climate or situation, then it is likely not worth its weight on the bike. Blending on and off the bike functionality is key to a compact, versatile, and sometimes even stylish wardrobe on the road.

An important skill to learn when dealing with a limited wardrobe is how to layer clothes effectively. Using a good layering system helps you carry less while being prepared for a variety of weather conditions, and also allows you to adjust on the go. Each of the three primary layers has a specific function. The base layer provides moisture management and some warmth or sun protection. The middle layer is an insulating layer that protects you from the wind and cold. The outer layer shields you from wind, rain, and snow.

Base Layer (Moisture Management)

The base layer is key to moving moisture (sweat) from your body. A good base layer is crucial to comfort in the outdoors. It helps prevent hypothermia in cold conditions and overheating in warm conditions.

The amount of base-layer coverage is purely up to you, and will likely be dictated by your touring destination and season. An ideal base layer is a light-weight, half-zip, long-sleeve, merino wool shirt. This will protect from the sun, provide a little warmth, and is excellent for managing moisture.

When it comes to fabric options, remember "cotton kills." Cotton isn't an ideal choice for touring clothes because it does not wick moisture, dry quickly, or repel odor. This makes you colder. Better alternatives are merino wool, silk blends, or a synthetic shirt (some trade names are Capilene, Coolmax, Zeoline, and PowerDry) as your base layer. A base layer isn't just a bike jersey or shirt; long underwear, underwear, and sports bras are considered base layers and require the same considerations when selecting fabrics.

Synthetics

Pros:

Very good moisture management

Quick drying time

Cheaper than wool

Durable; available in various weights and thicknesses for different conditions

Cons:

Get stinky over time; difficult to get rid of the smell even when you wash it

Petroleum-based material

Can feel irritating to skin when dirty

Merino Wool

Pros:

Offers good moisture management

Warm even when wet

Excellent odor resistance

Natural, soft on the skin (don't think of your Grandma's old-fashioned itchy wool sweater)

Comes in various weights and thicknesses for different conditions

Can repel light rain

Stretches

Sustainable

Ultraviolet resistant

Cons:

Expensive

A little less durable than synthetic clothes

Silk

Pros:

Decent at wicking moisture

Good for cold-weather use

Cons:

Pricey

Not the most durable

Not great for odor resistance

Slow to dry and not usually machine washable

Wool T-shirts such as these from Ibex and Icebreaker are ideal for long days on the bike and casual days off, here spent exploring islands off the coast of Thailand. BETH PULITI

Tip on wool: After years of use with the full gamut of fiber choices, merino wool comes out as the clear winner for a daily-worn base layer, and other garments when available. Its combination of comfort and performance for moisture management and odor elimination are unmatched. Traveling with limited garments will inevitably result in a less than appealing smell. Forget synthetic wicking garments, cotton Ts, technical base layers, and everything else with claims to performance. For everyday garments on and off the bike, merino wool offers superior properties for odor resistance, wicking performance, and drying speed with above average durability.

Tip: Arm warmers and knee or leg warmers are compact, lightweight, and versatile for adding warmth to your basic warm-weather attire. They are lightweight and easily packable and can be thrown on or taken off quickly and without removing your shoes.

Bottom Layer

Since you'll be in the saddle for much of the day, a pair of padded bike shorts in the clothing kit is inevitable for most touring cyclists. Options include standard Lycra bike shorts, bib shorts, liners, or baggy casual-style shorts. Whatever you choose, it is nice to have a casual pair of shorts for spending time in town and while off the bike. You can get away with carrying just two pairs of bike shorts regardless of the tour duration by cleaning and alternating them daily.

Insulating Layer/Mid-layer

The insulating layer, or mid-layer, is a versatile layer that's key to the layering system. It can be another wool wicking garment or a down- or synthetic-filled jacket, depending on the conditions. There are a number of options for mid-layers: fleece, natural fibers such as wool or down, or synthetic materials.

Fleece

Fleece comes in many thicknesses (weights) and is fairly inexpensive. It insulates when wet and is breathable. However, wind can whip through it and it is bulky and not very packable.

Natural Fibers

Natural fibers, including wool and down, can be an excellent choice for a mid-layer. Your mid-layer can be a wool jersey, or in colder climates a down jacket. Down jackets come in various weights and thicknesses just as sleeping bags do, allowing you to choose your mid-layer based on the condition, season, and temperature. Down has the best warmth-to-weight ratio and compressibility, but you don't want a down jacket to get wet because it loses its

It is easier and takes less calories to stay warm than to warm up. It's a good idea to throw on an extra layer or jacket when you stop riding and before you actually start feeling chilly.
JUSTIN LICHTER

insulative properties. Depending on your use and conditions, you may want a synthetic-fill jacket instead of down.

Synthetic

Synthetic jackets also come in different fill weights for different conditions. They are usually slightly heavier than down jackets, but they insulate better when wet and can stand up to repetitive wear underneath a backpack better. A synthetic layer can be a great layer underneath your rain jacket and provide extra warmth on a cold, wet day.

Wearing extra layers to stay warm in camp while cooking dinner with a multi-fuel stove in the Himalayas. JUSTIN LICHTER

Garments made from Windstopper fabric are a nice option because they block the wind and are warm, but as with most synthetic options they are bulkier and less compressible.

Outer Layer (Wind and Weather Protection)

The shell or outer layer is crucial since it protects you from wind, rain, and snow. It should keep your inner layers from getting wet and retain a proper level of body heat. A shell layer that doesn't breathe adequately can leave you just as wet on the inside because of condensation and sweat. The main considerations in a shell layer are weight, durability, waterproof laminate, DWR, and breathability. The other basic features like cut, pockets, pit zips, and hood should also be considered. There are four main types of shell layers: waterproof and breathable, water-resistant and breathable, waterproof and nonbreathable, and insulated.

Waterproof/Breathable Shells

These are the typical hard shells and are the most functional for touring. With a hard shell you are prepared for inclement weather conditions, while still maintaining a fairly light weight. When traveling with a bikepacking or lightweight touring setup, you'll need to consolidate clothing as much as possible.

Rather than carrying a separate windproof layer and rain shell, you can minimize your load by relying on a waterproof/breathable rain shell for weather protection, wind protection, and warmth.

Most hard shells are laminated or coated with waterproofing like Gore-Tex, eVent, or Neoshell. Some hard shells are geared toward skiing and mountaineering. They are made of heavier materials and can be more abrasion-resistant and have more features, but can be much heavier than a hard shell designed for biking.

Water-Resistant/Breathable Shells

These are known as soft shells or wind shells. They are best for mild weather, light precipitation, and high activity-level sports. Soft shells are breathable while wind shells aren't breathable, but neither handles precipitation as well as a hard shell. Most soft shells use some stretch material, which allows for good mobility, but they often don't pack as well as other options.

Waterproof/Nonbreathable Shells

These are more economical but don't breathe at all because they are designed for less active pursuits like fishing. While the inexpensive price may be tempting, this type of shell is a poor choice for cycling, since it will leave you just as wet on the inside from your own sweat.

Insulated Shells

Some shells have a built-in insulation layer designed for less aerobic activities. This sounds appealing since it essentially offers two garments in one, but an insulated shell is far less versatile then a concise layering system for touring and bikepacking. Keeping your insulation and waterproof shell separate also ensures your insulation layer remains dry and can be used inside your tent.

Rain Gear

Rain gear is an important part of your layering system. It provides protection from the elements. Good rain gear for biking must also be breathable, durable, and packable. With rain gear little things can make a big difference, so look for features like vents, pockets, and a hood to keep you comfortable when the weather turns foul.

Ventilation is key when cycling in rain gear; look for front zippers to vent a rain jacket, since this provides the most airflow when on the bike. Pit zips are another commonly available feature on active outdoor rain jackets, but for cycling they do not provide quite as much airflow since they are not directly in the wind.

A brightly colored rain jacket will keep you visible even on gray days. BETH PULITI

One area where some rain jackets skimp on quality is with poorly designed wrist cuffs. Some cuffs absorb water, staying wet longer than the rest of the jacket. Wet wrist cuffs also make you colder, since they cool down the blood flowing to your hands.

Tip: Look for a shell jacket equipped with a hood, and make sure it will fit over your bike helmet. A covered head will provide significantly more comfort when you are dealing with 8 hours of riding in the rain.

Tip: If you're below a tree line and it starts to rain, find a good tree to take shelter under. Open up your bag and get your rain gear on. The tree will keep you and your gear from getting soaked while you are suiting up.

Laminates
The waterproof laminates and coatings on rain gear often wear out quicker than the fabrics and materials themselves. As soon as the materials start to get dirty and worn they can leak. The first places that typically get roughed up on rain gear are the shoulders, if they are in regular contact with a pack's shoulder straps and hip belt.

Rain jackets have an inner waterproof layer and are categorized by their layers as two-layer, two-and-a-half-layer, and three-layer rain jackets.

Two-layer jackets are the most affordable. But they're not the most practical for long trips. They're usually a little heavier and less breathable. They're designed more as lifestyle jackets and for less frequent use.

Two-and-a-half-layer jackets are the lightest weight full-featured water-proof, breathable jackets. They can be well-priced, and have either coatings or laminates.

Three-layer rain jackets are the most durable. They're full-featured jackets that are highly breathable. These jackets have laminates and are usually more expensive.

There's not a good, universally accepted standard for fabric breathability that you will see often and on every product. Sometimes a tag might have a number in tens of thousands for waterproofness and breathability (like 30,000/30,000). Not all jackets have the numbers, though, and when they do it is usually geared more toward skiing and snowboarding jackets.

A lot of people debate about the effectiveness of waterproof fabric, such as eVent versus Gore-Tex laminates. No waterproof jacket ever breathes as much as you hope for; however, we have found eVent to be a bit better than Gore-Tex, but this can come at the cost of durability. We've seen eVent last a long time in stuff sacks, but we have also seen rain jackets with eVent leak after extended use. This happens eventually with any waterproof/breathable jacket, but it might happen a little quicker with eVent.

Seam Tape
Rain gear should be seam-taped. In the backcountry anything less is unacceptable—rain gear won't keep you dry, warm, or safe otherwise. The purpose of seam tape is to block puncture holes created by sewing needles when the jacket is made, so it plays an important role in keeping you dry and that can prevent hypothermia.

Weight
Rain jackets vary in weight from about 5 to 6 ounces, but can increase notably from there. Most 9- to 10-ounce shells are pretty solid, last a long time, and have sufficient features like pockets and vents. Rain gear designed for mountaineering and rugged off-trail travel usually weighs more than rain gear designed for biking. Jackets with fewer features like pockets and zippers usually weigh less.

Fit
Keep in mind many active-outdoor rain jackets have a trim, athletic cut. You'll want to examine the fit to ensure you have sufficient room to add a mid-layer on a cold rainy day. Also remember your position while cycling is stretched out compared to most outdoor sports. To accommodate this, cycling-specific rain jackets have longer arms and an extended tail in the rear, so these are an ideal choice if available.

Hoods

Look for a hood that fits over your bike helmet and can cinch down so it doesn't blow off when riding. Make sure it keeps the elements from entering and traveling to your base layers by going down your collar. Some jackets have hoods that stash in the collar or are detachable if you are using the jacket as a windbreaker as well. For pure wet-weather use, though, a fixed and well-fitting hood is indispensable and allows you to easily keep your upper body dry.

Vents

The biggest and best vent on any coat is the front zipper; it lets the most air in. Some pockets double as vents because they have a mesh liner. Vents in the armpits are also a popular feature that let in more air. But remember that each vent, pocket, bell, and whistle can add ounces to the jacket's weight.

Chin Guards

Some jackets have a chin guard, a piece of fabric or fleece on top of the zipper. It's a nice feature on a ski jacket, but it's not necessary on a rain jacket. On a wet rain jacket, fleece stays wet longer than the rest of the jacket. It becomes a cold piece of fabric to rest your chin on, like a sponge. However, a flap that covers the zipper's top is crucial—you don't want to get your chin or facial hair caught in the top of the zipper! Been there, done that, and don't ever want to do it again!

Storm Flap

Some rain jackets have a flap behind the main zipper to help keep wind and rain out. However, a jacket with a waterproof zipper doesn't need the flap, which can save some weight.

Pockets

More pockets equal a heavier jacket, and they are typically unnecessary when traveling by bike.

Drop Tail

Most biking rain gear should have a drop tail to prevent your butt from getting wet while you are riding. This is essential for a biking jacket.

Drawcords

Drawcords help cinch the rain jacket to the body to keep out snow, wind, and rain. A drawcord at the hem allows the wearer to cinch the jacket at the bottom. Biking rain gear doesn't need a powder skirt; a drawcord on the hem is enough for almost all conditions, and doesn't add the weight of a sprayskirt. Drawcords on the hood are key to cinch it down for a good, tight fit.

Tips on maintaining rain gear: Try to keep sunscreen and insect repellent (especially deet!) off your rain gear. Also, wash your rain gear occasionally. For eVent gear, hang-dry it. For Gore-Tex, put it in a dryer at low or medium heat for 10 minutes. Washing and drying helps the gear last longer because it removes dirt and the oils from your body that can diminish the performance of the waterproof breathable laminate or coating.

If you do put your rain gear into a dryer, make sure to remove it as soon as the time is up. Dryers remain hot after turning off; if your jacket settles on the wall and sits on a hot spot, it could melt.

Windbreakers and Vests

To remain comfortable and regulate your body temperature in a variety of climates, a windbreaker and/or lightweight vest can be a wonderful addition to your touring wardrobe. They rely on your own body heat to keep you warm by blocking wind from your core, which allows them to be extremely compact and lightweight. Look for a windbreaker with a fairly snug fit so it is not flapping in the wind as you ride. You can also wear it as a layer close to your core during chilly rainy days and colder weather when additional layers are required.

Tip: Although windbreakers are typically compact and lightweight, for bikepacking and ultralight touring you can save additional ounces by leaving them at home and relying on your rain shell as a wind barrier. On short trips when you are certain there is no rain in the forecast, leaving the rain gear at home and relying just on a windbreaker or vest will shave even more weight off your compact kit.

Socks

Socks are pretty important to having a good riding experience since they affect how your shoes fit, and can cause or prevent blisters or rubbing, so choose which socks you pack wisely.

Cycling socks come in a variety of heights, and are typically thin to provide a close and active fit between your shoe and pedal for maximum performance. In summer standard cycling socks help keep your feet cool and aid in wicking sweat. They are designed with performance, durability, abrasion resistance, warmth, cushioning, weight, wicking, height (low, ankle, mid-calf, knee-high), quick-drying capabilities, and odor repelling in mind.

Depending on the season and location, lightweight socks just over the ankle are the go-to. Carry one or two pairs and a pair of midweight socks as sleep socks, if you are camping. Using a heavier sock as a sleep sock helps you stay warm and comfortable at night. In colder weather you might want to upgrade your sock thicknesses by one level—midweight socks for riding and heavyweight socks for around the campsite and sleeping.

Sock Categories

Yes, there are distinct categories of socks. They range in thickness and purpose from liners, which are the thinnest, to heavy-duty socks for mountaineering, which are thick and as the name implies—heavy.

Liners

Liners are lightweight, thin socks meant to be worn under other socks. They are moisture wicking, can help alleviate hot spots, and can help shoes fit more comfortably while keeping your feet and socks from getting wet from sweaty feet. I have also worn liners as lightweight socks. They work but aren't as durable as other lightweight socks, since liners are designed for use underneath heavier socks that prevent the liners from getting any abrasions.

Lightweight Cycling Socks

These socks are made for warmer conditions and people who like less sock. Most cyclists use this level of sock or even a sock designed for running. They usually are geared toward pedaling performance and provide wicking benefits more than warmth. They are a little thicker than sock liners and more durable. Some brands add a little cushioning and abrasion resistance in key areas and use a thinner weave in other areas for breathability.

Midweight Socks

These are heavier with more cushioning than lightweight socks. Midweight socks are designed for use in average or cold temperatures, and also make for great all-around socks for those of us with more temperature-sensitive feet.

Mountaineering/Heavy-Duty Socks

These are the thickest socks around and not typically used for cycling, but you may want to carry a pair for camp socks since they will keep your feet warmer in your sleeping bag.

Materials

What a sock is made of dramatically affects its performance. It's not just wool or cotton anymore—many socks are made of a blend of materials for maximum performance.

Wool

Wool is a popular sock material for the same reasons it is preferred for base layers and other clothing. Wool is comfortable, wicks moisture, repels odor, and stays warm when wet. It can take a little longer than synthetic materials to dry and can be less durable, so some socks are made from a wool blend to compensate for these negatives.

Synthetic Materials

Many companies use synthetic materials for socks because they last longer and dry faster. An example of synthetics is a trade name like Coolmax, which is commonly used in cycling socks.

Cotton

As with clothing, cotton is not an ideal material for your cycling socks. It absorbs moisture, doesn't insulate well, gets dirty fast, and can lead to blisters.

Other Materials

Many socks also have other materials woven into them to increase certain properties. For example, most socks have nylon or Lycra woven in to increase stretch and shape retention.

Cushioning

Some cycling socks provide cushioning in certain areas of the sock, like the heel and ball of the foot, by increasing the density of the weave in those key areas. The added cushioning can increase comfort provided the fit of your shoes is not compromised. You can also consider adding cushion to your feet by replacing the stock insole of your cycling shoes with an aftermarket option.

Sock-drying tip: Put socks and other damp materials in your sleeping bag at night to dry them. To prevent wet socks from freezing in cold weather, put them between your bag and your sleeping pad. You can also attach wet socks to your seatpost bag or rear rack so that they dry throughout the day while you are riding.

Shoes

Footwear for bikepacking or a bike tour can vary depending on the type of riding you are doing and if you are bringing along a second pair of shoes for off the bike time. On the bike a shoe that is clipped into your pedals offers unmatched efficiency, but walking around town in them, particularly road shoes, can be an annoyance. If you'll be spending a lot of time doing off the bike sightseeing, then a single pair of comfortable sneakers combined with toe clips or flat pedals can save you from packing an extra pair of town shoes or wearing your bike shoes around town. Whenever pedaling any notable distance, though, I prefer the performance of cycling-specific shoes and being clipped into my pedals. If the tour is with a lightweight bikepacking setup, then camp shoes typically don't make the cut. On longer bike tours packing along off the bike shoes or sandals brings comfort that's worth the extra weight.

Appendix: Gear Checklist

Here's a generic checklist to use as a guide for an overnight adventure if you're scrambling to pack up and get out the door. It can of course be catered to the season, destination, and type of tour/bikepacking trip, but you'll find it to be a useful reference tool for gathering your gear.

Quick Gear Checklist

Item	Weight	✓
Carrying System		
Panniers		
Frame bag, seat bag, handlebar bag		
Hydration pack/backpack		
Sleep System		
Sleeping bag		
Sleeping pad		
Shelter and tent stakes		
Groundsheet		
Clothing		
Bike shorts		
T-shirt, base layer, or cycling jersey		
Socks		
Mid-layer/insulating layer		
Rain pants		
Rain jacket and/or wind jacket		
Underwear		
Casual clothes		
Arm warmers and knee warmers		
Accessories—shoes, helmet, cap, sunglasses		
Warm accessories—beanie, gloves, toe/shoe covers		

Food and Water		
Stuff sack (for food bag)		
Cookware (pot, stove, windscreen, spork, fuel, lighter)		
Plate, bowl or cup, and utensil(s)		
Water treatment		
Water bottle(s)		
Water bladder		
Snacks, dehydrated meals, drink mix, etc.		
Necessities and Accessories		
Map, book, notebook, trail info, knife, pen, spare batteries, first-aid kit, and media card for camera		
Toiletries (travel toothbrush, toothpaste, and floss, contact lens stuff, glasses, toilet paper, towel, etc.)		
Personal items—credit card, ID, keys (if necessary), cash		
Electronics—phone, camera, GPS, satellite tracker, etc.		
Repair kit—spare tubes, tire levers, duct tape, etc.		

Index

fabric breathability, 122
fleece, 91, 118–19
insulating (middle) layer, 118–19
laundry, 56
rain gear, 120–24
shells, 119–20
shoes, 127
socks, 124–26
windbreakers/vests, 124
cotton, 91, 115, 126
Couchsurfing, 55
cowboy camping, 51, 95
credit cards, 2, 9, 59–60
cross bike, 18
currency of foreign countries, 59–60
cyclocross bikes, 5, 12

daypacks, 79
debit cards, 59–60
desert camping, 51
diesel fuel, 102
digital maps, 57
dinner options, 45–47
dirt roads. See gravel road touring
disc brakes, 11, 18, 23, 76
down clothing, 118–19
down sleeping bags, 88–89
dust, 15–16

electrolyte drinks, 47–48
esbit tablet, 98
eVent, 122, 124
expedition kits, 84

fat bikes, 20–21
filters, 108, 109, 110
flat tires, 16
fleece, 91, 118–19
foam pads, 94
folding bikes, 7–8

food
carrying, 25
options for, 43–47
quick checklist, 129
shopping for, 16, 25, 68, 79
frame bags, 10, 15, 21, 31–32, 34–35
full suspension, 19–20, 22

gasoline, 102, 103
gear
balancing, 10
long-distance, 76–78
organizing for weather
problems, 27
quick checklist, 128–29
weight considerations, 24, 31–36
See also clothing; food; off-bike
gear; sleeping bags; stoves;
water treatment
Giardia, 107
Gore-Tex, 122, 124
GPS units, 57
gravel road touring
additional considerations, 15–18
bike selection, 12–13
carrying methods, 14–15, 16–18
restocking options, 16
tires, 16
group adventures, 38–39

handlebar bags, 16–18, 32, 33–34
handlebars, 11, 24, 77
hand position, 11
hardtails, 19–20, 22
headlamps, 113–14
highway riding, 63
honking by drivers, 65
hotels, 53
hydration packs, 30–31
hydraulic disc brakes, 23

waterproof/breathable shells, 119–20

waterproof/nonbreathable shells, 120

water-resistant/breathable shells, 120

water sources
campsite selection and, 50
carrying, 25
finding, 47–48
international considerations, 71
quick checklist, 129

water treatment
chemical options, 109, 111
contaminants, 107
evaluation of options, 109

filters, 108, 109, 110
purification, 108–10
SteriPEN, 111–12
taste of water and, 107–8

weather problems, 27, 80
See also outer layer of clothing

weight considerations, 24, 31–36, 122

wheel size, 10, 18, 20, 72–73

white gas, 101–2, 103

wild camping, 49–52, 71

windbreakers/vests, 124

wood-burning stoves, 98

wool, 115, 116, 117, 118, 126

zippers on sleeping bags, 92–93

About the Authors

Justin Lichter has hiked more than 35,000 miles since 2002, including thru-hikes on the Appalachian Trail, International AT, Eastern Continental Trail, Pacific Crest Trail, Pacific Northwest Trail, Continental Divide Trail, and Great Divide Trail, as well as treks in the southern Alps, New Zealand, Africa, Iceland, and the Himalaya Range. He is a "Triple Crowner," having hiked the ECT, PCT, and CDT (more than 10,000 miles) in one year. Check him out at justinlichter.com.

    Justin Kline has pedaled loaded bicycles tens of thousands of miles. While he prefers the dirt and solitude of the wilderness, that hasn't stopped him from exploring some of the busiest cities around the globe on two wheels. Whether on the Great Divide, at home in New Hampshire's White Mountains, or in an olive grove halfway around the world, his best rides end under the stars with nothing more than what was carried on his bicycle. Justin currently works remotely while pedaling on an open-ended international bike tour.